CHICKEN / TURKEY BEEF PORK SEAFOOD

■TIP: Green-Color means OTHER.■ - Means 3 different kinds of meats can

TIME FOR SIDES! RECIPES FROM ALL OF US!...
- ■ Magical Amazing Coleslaw - (It truly is!)...107
- ▌TACO MANIA SALAD! (Where is tequila at?)..110
- ■ OH MY CABBAGE! Red Cabbage Salad. UGH so good!.................................113
- ■ CRABSTER (For the sea lovers) Super darn quick crab meat salad!..............115
- ■ Polish Kopytka (Sort of like gnocchi kind of better) 117
- ■ The David-Mash – Potatoes!...119
- ■ Garlic-zilla Fries..122
- ■ Vienna Sausage Rice Delight!...125
- ■ Fried Brussels Sprouts!...127

NOW ITS TIME FOR A CHAPTER DEDICATED TO MY SISTER AND HER RECIPES! SEA-LOVERS THIS ONE'S FOR YOU.. 129
- ■ SCALLOPS LA LOCA - Don't worry you won't go crazy after.......................130
- ■ Scary Monsters: Crab Legs...133
- ■ The Grand Baked Oysters! 136

IF YOU HAVE A BAD DAY TURN TO THIS PAGE ------------------------→......**139**

BACK TO MAIN DISHES..**140**
- ■ BBQ Ribsies..141
- ▌Polish Krokiety & Nalesniki 2 in 1 – Stuffed crepes..144
- ▌The Secret Buttermilk Chick'n-ZILLA Sandwich...148
- ■ Home-Made David's Margherita Pizza...151
- ■ Great Mongolian Beef..154
- ▌Paprika Porkie In Creamy Sauce..157

DRINK MENU ...(Adults Only)...160

N
E
X
T

P
A
G
E

Appetizers

CHICKEN / TURKEY BEEF PORK SEAFOOD

■ TIP: Green-Color means OTHER. ■ - Means 3 different kinds of meats can be used for this dish.

APPETIZERS..161
■ Blooming Onion..162
■ Avocadonator Devilled Eggsies..164
■ JALAPENO CHEESE BALLZ – NO BAKING NEEDED...165
■ The Chipster Dip..167
■ Them Chick'n Sliders..168
■ The Avocado Emperor Toast...170

IT IS THE END CHAPTER...**171**

DISCLAIMER:
Never trust people who renovate kitchens -they specialize in counterfeiting. Of course this is just a joke;) I had to have a last run!

Dear Chef:
Just like that, you ended up here. The end of the cooking frontier. How was it? *Good? Bad?* I hope *good.* Thank you for purchasing this book. I hope you improved your mediocre cooking skills. Now you can impress your friends, spouse, gf, bf, your dog... etc... *Also, now you know that if your sibling or friend still thinks that the only vegetable/fruit that can make them cry is an onion. Throw a coconut at them and ask again.* You are welcome.

THE End!

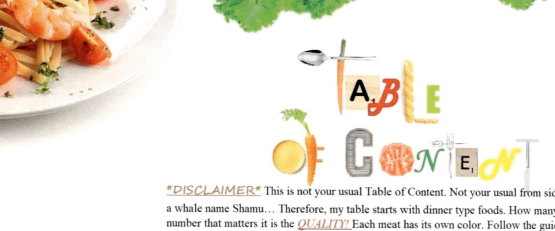

Table of Content

DISCLAIMER This is not your usual Table of Content. Not your usual from sides to dessert style. I am like a whale name Shamu… Therefore, my table starts with dinner type foods. How many recipes? Well, it is not the number that matters it is the *QUALITY!* Each meat has its own color. Follow the guide below.

🟩 TIP: Green-Color means OTHER. 🟥 - Means 3 different kinds of meats can be used for this dish.

CHICKEN / TURKEY   **BEEF**   **PORK**   **SEAFOOD**

Introduction..1
About the Autor..2
Abbreviations...3
MAIN DISHES 4

🟧 The Sexy Tuscan Shrimp – oh he sexy! *(Pasta)*..................................5
🟧 Cajun Shrimpster *(Shrimp & Rice)*..8
🟧 The Naked Shrimp *(Shrimp & Rice)*...11
🟧 Shrimp of Troy! Mediterranean style *(Pasta)*....................................14

THAT'S ENOUGH OF SHRIMP! MAIN DISHES TIME! DO NOT WORRY THIS IS NOT THE END OF SEAFOOD...17

🟥 Ziti Witty Meatballs... 18
🟥 Cajun & Bacon Madness *(Pasta)* 21
🟪 Dijon Pork Chopsies (Banging porkchops!)...............24
🟨 Crispy Chipotle Honey Chick'n.................................27
🟨 OPA Chicken Gyro – For the Greek lovers!.............31
🟩 Loaded Stuffed Shells – Easy Breezy!...................... 35
🟥 Grand Imperium Lasagna – Cheesy and beautiful like you!... 38
🟨 Fried Chick'n! Fingerlicious! - Kind of like you!.... buy me a dinner first.. 41
🟨 Stone Fire (hot hot) Chicken veggie naan!...............44
🟫 Beijing Beef – Spicy, delicious, sensational!.............47
🟨 Quick Chick'n Parmesan!... 50

CHICKEN / TURKEY　　BEEF　　PORK　　SEAFOOD

■ TIP: Green-Color means OTHER. ■ - Means 3 different kinds of meats can be used for this dish.

WELCOME TO MOM AND HER RECIPES!..52

■ Mom's style authentic Polish Golombki………Eng. Stuffed cabbage rolls………..53
■ Authentic Polish Pierogi! None of that BS kind! Real from my mom!......................57
■ Polish Placki Ziemniaczane (Potato pancakes) Effin delicious!................................61

OUR SOUPS TIME! Family chapter. Mom, me, grandma and sister. All in one!..65

■ My SOUP of the day is: *Not So Shy Tomato Soup! Traditional!*......................66
■ Mom's SOUP of the day is: *Chicken DOODLE DOO Soup! Traditional!*......69
■ Grandma's SOUP of the day is: *Holy-Moly Pickle Soup! Traditional!*............72
■ My Sister's SOUP of the day is: *Crazy CRAB! SOUP!*....................................75

RECIPES FOR THE GRILL - SEASON BEGINS!...78

■ Brown sugar bourbon grill explosion chick'n!..... **works for oven too**……………….79
■ Grilled Steak (Livin' La Vida Loca)………………………………………………….82
■ Avocado Glazed Salmon - Straight of your grill! -Your mom likes it, at least that is what she told me….85
■ Super Loaded Baked Summer Potatoes from the grill! - What a long name……………………………….88
■ THE BURGERZILLA! – best burger ever. **Can also be done on the stove!**.......................91

CHAPTER DEDICATED TO MY BEAUTIFUL GRANDMOTHER AND HER TRADITIONAL RECIPES!............94

■ Kotlety Mielone – don't even try to pronounce it – Polish meat ovals……………95
■ Authentic Polish Pierogi with meat- Not that BS kind…………………………..98
■ Schabowe Dinner! – Polish pork chops…………102

M
O
R
E

R
E
C
I
P
E
S

NEXT PAGE

INTRODUCTION

Okay, so is this a real useful Cookbook?

Judging by the cover one might think this is a big ole joke! I know I get that a lot every time someone looks at me... But it is not. This is a real useful cookbook. It is a little bit unusual like me and probably first of its kind! Trust me! It is bit hilarious... sometimes ridiculous - but totally useful. *Disclaimer* you might get F-up while following some recipes!

What is in this Cookbook?

Amazing, delicious recipes filled with loads of *sh*t and giggle humor!* Also, some motivation! If you are ready to buckle up & take a shot after a long damn day while laughing your buttocks off while cooking - then this book was made just for someone like you. This wonderful book has recipes that came from my heart also contains recipes from my sister, mother and grandmother! How family oriented! Recipes that are Internationally mixed, some made up and some accidental gems! Do not worry, all tested will not get you stranded in the bathroom. If some do, please stock up on paper like its Coronavirus... Too soon? Ops... Please do not leave yet. Wanna hear a poop joke? Nah, they always stink.

What is the purpose of this book?

The idea behind this was to introduce a different type of cookbook that not only gets your dinner ready but also loosens up your Botox a bit. It is filled with my humor. Sometimes dry, sometimes totally cringey and at times totally funny! I am like a stand-up comedian in the kitchen... I already know how to stand up... Still waiting for comedy to follow along though. Okay, let us continue to TACO about this book. This book is meant to be a real cookbook that does work! But can also be utilized as a gag gift. The material is RAW ... just like the beef you are about to use. Man, did I lose you yet? No? GREAT! That means this book is for you. Now go to the store grab some liquor of choice or juice box if preferred and LET'S GET GOING! But remember... *DON'T BURN IT!*

Disclaimer!

This book is not meant for people who cannot take a joke. Not for the easily offended. If you are one of these above, then we are not a match. See sort of like a dating app you tell me what you do not like, and I swipe left to tell you bye.

Pg.1

About the Author

My name is **David Skrzypczyk-Cole (Originally Dawid Skrzypczyk)** You are probably going like ''How the F do you even procurance that '' looks like you slammed your hand on the keyboard and called it a ''last name'' I get it. Had to change the W into V once moved to USA as W is a V where I came from. Quite complicated huh. I also added Cole to my last name to make it little easier! I was born in Poland, for those non geographical specimens that's Central Europe and if you do not know where Europe is then well, I recommend buying a map... I popped out into this world on *August 29, 1994.* Moved to the United States of America in the early 2005. Before you try to deport me or tell me to move back to my country, I am a proud citizen of United States. So good try! I had moved and traveled a lot in my short little life. I lived in few places in two different continents. I changed schools like your friend changes girlfriends. I explored the world and cuisine of few countries I lived in, and other ones I traveled to. I lived in places like North and South Poland, London – England, In the United States places like:

Jersey City, Roselle Park – New Jersey, East Stroudsburg – Pennsylvania, Los Angeles – California, Boynton Beach - Florida.

I hope I have not missed any! Some places I moved back to more than once! All that travel made me discover many cuisines around! On my travels I always try authentic food in every country/place I visit. I have met many friends around the globe that introduced me to their food and opened my mind to be who I am today. This is not a professional ''About the author'' you are used to. Where, we brag about things we accomplished and so on. This is an authentic take on who I am, so while reading this you can sort of get to know me. Well, hello there! Nice to meet you. I am David! This is my first work that will be published, and I am immensely proud of this. I hope your humor matches mine a little bit and you will enjoy this piece of work like I did while writing it. Have you ever laughed at your own jokes? I sure did while writing this. There is one motto in life, do what you think is impossible and laugh at everything while doing so. Special thanks to my sister Sylvia, my mom Dorota, and my grandma Teresa for giving me some of their special recipes they have either created or passed through many generations of our family existence. My recipes were either ''let me make something from what I have left in the kitchen'' or simple '' experiments'' that ended up delicious! Not to brag but they truly are! I hope that this book will make you giggle! Thank you from the bottom of my heart for purchasing this book. You are not only supporting my idea but also make me feel like nothing is impossible. Yes, as a reader you have that power. Please enjoy this material! Share with friends. Once you are done! Why not pass it down!

Abbreviations

-Basically a useful cheat sheet for the first-time chefs! Did I use all of them in the book? Well, no, not really. However, why not know this for future. Let us be honest you will probably never use this page, and if you do *WELL HELLO THERE!* You deserve a shot for even turning to this page.

Some recipes use the following abbreviations:

C .... cup
lb/lbs .... pound
oz .... ounce
pkg .... package
pt .... pint
qt .... quart
Tbsp/Tbs .... tablespoon
tsp .... teaspoon

ALSO:
GET THIS = Ingredients.
DO THIS = Steps.

The Sexy Tuscan Shrimp

About the dish:

Tuscan? I know, I am talking rubbish here *(for our non-cultural cookers rubbish means garbage in England)*. This is NOT a traditional recipe form Tuscany… not passed from a cute little Italian grandma - *I know disappointing*. It is sort of inspired and sort of nailed kind of recipe. Paired with nice wine and it is like you are outside in beautiful Tuscany…Then you get a glimpse of reality and bam… you are eating this in your …crappy kitchen with shi*ty weather outside. That does not mean you cannot dream right? Anyways, this is really a delicious dish! Great for summer! It is not difficult so give it a go! You will not be disappointed.

Pg.5

Serving: Normally 4... I really do not know how much you eat so cannot guarantee it is 4.

Prep Time: 5 minutes. I hate this one... I mean normally takes 5 mins... Anyone really follows this?

Cook time: 20 minutes. Unless you are Chuck Norris...

Get This:

2 tablespoons salted butter -#DadJokeOfTheDay - *Did you hear the joke about the butter? What is it?* I cannot tell you; you will spread it.

1-pound cooked (500 g) shrimp (or prawns), tails off, - Kids always tell you the truth. I was at the store, this kid behind me said to his dad: *Mama's so big, it took me two buses and a train to get to her good side.* Man, I never laughed so hard...

READ THE NEXT ONE OUT LOUD!

1 SMALL *(just like your bf or husband)* **yellow onion diced** - Now Quiet! *(You said Small .... now your husband does not know if you are talking about this onion or him... You lock eyes... It is awkward ... Guess you are not getting laid tonight Linda.)* My bad!

1 3/4 cups half and half *(Half milk half not... Just like you right now after insulting your loved one's size... half wife half divorced).* Mic drops.

6 cloves garlic finely diced - Lady at a Mc'D's got really annoyed with the kid sitting next to her. She got up went over to the mom and said: *Your kid is so annoying he makes his Happy Meal cry.*

5 oz (150 g) jarred sun dried tomato strips in oil, drained *(reserve 1 teaspoon of the jarred oil for cooking)* Don't let me start on this... If you do not like Sun Dried tomatoes, how are we even friends ... *We are not?* well sucks for you.

Salt and pepper — My friend got into a fight with her husband and said: *You are so stupid, when they said, "Order in the court," you asked for fries and a shake.* He replied: *Your cooking is so nasty, flys got together and fixed the hole in the window screen.* Results of a 10+ marriage.

2/3 cup fresh grated Parmesan cheese – I remember one time I went to a dinner at friend's house. His grandpa asked him if he knew what is the difference between an EGG and him... He asked what... his grandpa responded... *Egg gets laid – you do not.* I almost swallowed my spoon laughing. What a savage beast!

2 teaspoons dried Italian herbs - Dried Italian... sounds like my best friend's grandpa *Giuseppe*.

3 cups baby spinach leaves washed — Funny story, I hear this kid in front of me say this to the other one... *Yo mama is so fat, when she fell, I did not laugh, but the sidewalk cracked up.* What a savage little sh*t.

1 teaspoon of flour - Put the straw down. This isn't MIAMI!

Pg.6 **1 tablespoon fresh parsley chopped** – Did something died in here? Oh, yeah your style did.

DO THIS:

IF you want this to be served over pasta, boil one package in water once done drain-set aside. Heat up that LARGE skillet over medium-high heat *(Don't say large out loud as we both know after the last comment it is not the hubby)*. Melt the salty butter and add in the garlic and fry until fragrant *(about one minute, that is like 15 pushups? or if you are a beach whale like me that is 2 steps to the fridge and back)*. Add in the shrimp and fry two minutes on each side, until just cooked through and pink. Transfer to a bowl; set aside.

FRY our onion in the butter remaining in the skillet *(if you wear mascara cover your eyes, unless you want to serve dinner looking like a wet racoon)*. Pour in the white wine *(if using)* - *of course you are I have seen you at the AA meeting last Sunday... Y are lying like this*. Moving on, allow to reduce to half, while scraping any bits off the bottom *(do not scrap your son please not that kind of bottom)* of the pan. Add the sun-dried tomatoes and fry for 1-2 minutes to release their flavors. *(At least something has flavors... yours EXPIRED already)*.

REDUCE heat to low-medium heat, add the half and half and bring to a gentle simmer, while stirring occasionally. Season with salt and pepper to your taste. <-- *See I can sound professional but WHY would I though,* OKAY CONTINUE!

ADD in the spinach leaves and allow to wilt in the, add in parmesan cheese. Allow sauce to simmer for a further minute until cheese melts through the sauce. (For a thicker sauce, add the milk/cornstarch mixture to the center of the pan, and continue to simmer while quickly stirring the mixture through until the sauce thickens.) Add the shrimp back into the pan; sprinkle with the herbs and parsley and stir through.

SERVE over pasta, rice or steamed veg. Or some other crappy option of yours because you are on diet, or food intolerant or some other Foodie - free chooser. Why do not you just eat an ICE CUBE instead.... Sure, do not follow the damn recipe why would you...

*Disclaimer – It is the first recipe, do not call the manager on me…take a shot and shut up. *

Quick Game!
Finish the drawing.
Draw anyone that pisses you off.
Yes it can be your spouse.

Pg. 7

Cajun Shrimpster

About the dish:

Well, look where we are now! Cajun shrimp.. *Kind of spicy?* I mean, I will not lie, this dish hits the spot! It is quite easy – therefore, if you were shit*ing bricks right now going like ''*I cannot cook!*'' Calm the hell down… Even if you have two left hands and cannot cook at all, this dish is a solution to your serious struggles. *You want to impress someone?* Make this recipe a reality. *Who knows might get you laid!* Cajun cuisine is a style of cooking developed by the Cajun–Acadians who were deported from Acadia to Louisiana during the 18th century. *OKAY!* See this book wont only capture your heart but also teach you some history! *Now you are 1 pound heavier and 1 pound smarter!* Also, before I forget this dish originated in my kitchen with a hint of inspiration. Okay, let's go!

Get This:

Serving: 4 adults, probably one dog…

Pep Time: 15 minutes!

Cook Time: 15 Minutes! Unless you screw it up. Then maybe more!

1 ⅓ cups uncooked long grain white rice – Listen guys! I am going to start my own brand of rice wine called *"Shi Kitsune"* - Of course we will have to translate it for the US market, *Four Fox Sake*. Get it? No? Okay… I tried!

1-pound large shrimp peel tails of if needed – #DadJokeOfTheDay - Why should a banana go to the doctor? He does not peel well! Ha-ha! No?!? I try… Give me some damn credit!

2 ⅔ cup chicken broth – For the mathematically broken specimens... 2/3 translates to… Go to the damn store and buy measuring cups!

1 teaspoon minced garlic – My grandpa goes the other day. David what does garlic and Uncle Chuck have in common? I go… *what*!? Grandpa: *They both stink.* - I am glad that despite the age my grandpa can still throw some shade!

4 tablespoons butter – Melt it! Usually, microwave works. If you do not have one… Idk breath on it. Figure it out!

WHAT TO GET FOR CAJUN SEASONING?

1 teaspoon salt – I thought id be precise! Since saying ''pinch of salt'' usually ends up in disaster because you are clumsy, and your taste buds already expired. You are very welcome!

1 ½ teaspoons paprika - If you do not own a damn teaspoon then you need to get your life together Karen! Sean! Whatever your name is.

½ teaspoon cracked black pepper – Cracked… Just like your damn back!

1 teaspoon garlic powder – This one will be dark… Buckle up! My mom always said garlic powder makes everything better so when I was little, I sprinkled some on my parents' marriage certificate. You guessed they divorced. Did not make it better! Quite the opposite!

½ teaspoon onion powder – I always loved onions. To the point my family nickname when I was a child was fuck*ng ONION!

½ teaspoon dried oregano – Dried, just like your love life! Ops!

¼ teaspoon crushed red pepper flakes - Spicy! Like me! Rawr.

½ teaspoon cayenne pepper – Just that. See I can be quite professional!

Do This:

OKAY, you finally decided to take this dish for a spin! Okay well, let us get going! Whisk together all the ingredients for the Cajun seasoning. *MIX, MIX, MIX!*

TAKE your butter and please melt 2 tablespoons in a large skillet over medium heat. Now please stir in garlic, half of the Cajun seasoning you have made, and the uncooked rice. You might go *''Oh well David you are being quite polite today! WOW''* Yes, I am also super surprised!

SINCE we are being so polite in this recipe! Please stir in chicken broth, bring to a boil, reduce to a simmer and cover. Cook for about solid 15 minutes, stirring 1-3 times throughout the process. How pleasant is this recipe? You also look beautiful! **Now you smile** Yes, I caught you!

MEANWHILE rice is cooking, prepare the shrimp by stirring together remaining 2 tablespoons melted butter and remaining Cajun seasoning. Then, pour over shrimp and toss to coat. *Toss that shrimp honey! Work it Bi*ch!* ← Man, here we go.

STIR shrimp into the rice, cover and cook 3-5 minutes longer until shrimp is pink and opaque. Garnish with chopped parsley! *Bon Appetite!* Now get fuc*ed up and eat!

Disclaimer: Hey you! Thank you for taking your time to make this. Are you satisfied? If **YES** – Great! If **NO** – Well bye to you too! This was supposed to be a disclaimer but whatever. *

Did you have a shot of liqour? Mark below.

I am a baddas Bi*ch

I prefer water.

Flip the book upside-down!

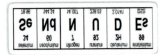

Please don't send them - this was just a joke.

After you flip this book upside-down
To reveal the message
Place mirror on the line.
Da-Vinci used this method.

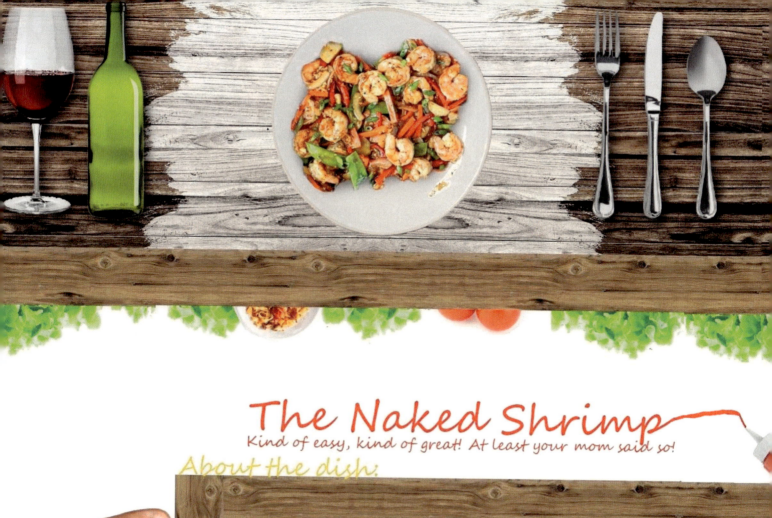

The Naked Shrimp
Kind of easy, kind of great! At least your mom said so!

About the dish:

Have you ever ordered Chinese takeout? Am I even asking... of course you did! When it comes to me, my whale butt orders food super late... Sometimes I am a beach whale in the bathtub soaking while eating food... *DON'T JUDGE ME...* Just keep swimming... Well, this dish is inspired by the Chinese shrimp in garlic sauce. It is yummy and easy *(Just like your uncle Joe)! JOKE!* Please, do not throw this book away! This might not be an exact spot-on imitation, but it is kind of good! I tried! If you give this a try – you are on path of adventure! *GO ON! DO IT! DO IT!* – Too much pressure? *SO, WHAT?!*

Pg.11

Serving: Who knows 3-4-5? I mean depends how hungry you are.

Prep Time: I guess 15 minutes?

Cook Time: Usually also 15 minutes. WHAT'S UP WITH ALL THESE QUESTIONS. What am I? Damn interned browser?!

Get This:

1 lb. large, cooked shrimp - Peeled, deveined and tails removed do not be too rough Rebecca! This is not 50 shades of GRAY!

3 tablespoons vegetable oil - If not, olive oil is always good... I mean let us be honest any oil will do. No judgment here!

1 Green, Red or Yellow - Or whatever color of the bell peppers you will find, who cares about color anyways! Make it multicultural and add 1/4 of each! Why not? Call it Mixmerica!

1/2 onion - This guy was claiming that onions are the only food that can make you cry. So I threw a coconut at his face. He changed his mind.

Some scallions for garnish.

1 large carrot - Peeled and cut into matchstick sizes or circles or whatever the heck shapes you are able to do.

5 cloves garlic - Rest in peace garlic, you will be minced! GET IT?

1/2 cup chicken stock - My friend to his wife: *Your butt is so big it has it's own zip code.* She quicly replied: *You are so fat not even Dora could explore you!* They are happily married!

1/8 cup soy sauce - For the non-mathematical specimens like me that is 2 tablespoons! hah.

1 tablespoon flour - Sit down SNIFFANY this is not Miami...

1/2 tablespoon white vinegar - I can't mess with vinegar... He's already a bitter Bi**h

1 1/2 tablespoon raw honey - This kid goes: *If laughter is the best medicine, your face must be curing the world.* Kids these days! Ouch.

1 cup sugar snap peas - Oh snap!

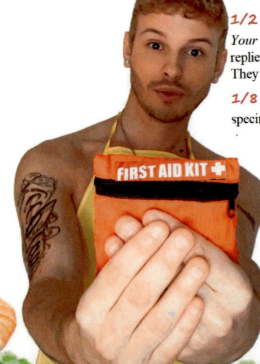

Do This!

IN A MEDIUM BOWL, throw in chicken stock, flour, vinegar *(be careful he is not easy)*, soy sauce, honey, and 2 tbs of garlic. Whisk until combined. Looks lovely, doesn't it? No? Why are you so hard to impress!

HEAT A LARGE CAST IRON SKILLET or heavy bottom pan *(no not you SEAN do not sit on the stove, this is not GRINDR, and you are not the heavy bottom we are looking for)* to medium high, add 1 tablespoon oil and add shrimp and cook for 2 minutes then flip and cook another 2 minutes. Remove and set aside. So far doing good!

NEXT ADD about 2 tablespoons of oil and add carrots *(I wonder what stupid shapes you chose this time)*, peas, onions, red peppers *(or your multicolor mix)*, cook 3-4 minutes until softened. Add water and 1tbs of garlic, cook another minute.

GIVE SAUCE another few whisks in the bowl to make sure the flour has not settled at the bottom. Then add it to the veggie mixture, reduce heat to low, add shrimp back in, stir and cook about another 2-5 minutes until thickened.

SERVE over rice, whichever kind really. No judgment unless you are weird, and you eat it with like. PASTA ... What are you doing with your life...? Scratch it .... Would that really be a bad idea thought?!?! O.O IDK Give it a try and let me know. **COOK RICE if using! DO NOT FORGRT ABOUT RICE! FOLLOW BOX INSTRUCTIONS!**

DISCLAIMER: * To those who got offended here is a tissue - *throws a box of tissues at you* – Also no Seans were harmed in this recipe. If your name happened to be Sean sorry to spill your secret out. *

How did you do?

I screwed up! ☐   I DID AMAAAZIN'! ☐

A	B	C	D	E	F	G	H	I	J	K	L	M
1	2	3	4	5	6	7	8	9	10	11	12	13

N	O	P	Q	R	S	T	U	V	W	X	Y	Z
14	15	16	17	18	19	20	21	22	23	24	25	26

Little game: Reveal secret message. Write each letter down according to the number.

20 15 14 9 7 8 20   9 19   25 15 21 18   14 9 7 8 20   7 5 20   3 18 1 26 25
7 5 20   23 1 19 20 5 4   25 15 21   4 5 19 5 18 22 5   9 20

Pg.13

Shrimp of TROY

About the dish:

Let me take you on an adventure to the Mediterranean Sea! Close your eyes! Imagine yourself on a yacht at the beautiful blue Mediterranean Sea! If your imagination sucks a*s turn on your portable fan *(to imitate sea wind),* put a bowl in a sink turn water on *(imitation of waves)* close your eyes and bam! You are there! Now let me bring you back to reality. Open your eyes… Ops its just your shit*y kitchen again! It is okay though with this dish we can sort of change that! Maybe I will not be able to take you on Mediterranean Sea, but I will let your stomach taste it! This dish is heavily inspired by that part of the world mentioned above! *Why Troy?* I wanted this dish to sound *MIGHTY!* Paired with wine, candle and bam! You have the sexiest dinner date with your loved one… or your cat! Whatever rolls with you! *Okay, lets go!*

Get This:

Serving: Well, about 4 human adults.
Prep Time: 10 minutes!
Cook Time: 10-15 minutes! WOW!

1 lb. large shrimp peeled and deveined (thawed if frozen) – Starting the recipe very dry! #DadJokeOfTheDay - Where do you go to buy and sell shrimp? The Prawn shop. *Bad?!?*

¾ lb. thin spaghetti – Oh my I swear today's kids are such savages! So, there is me minding my business at a restaurant. I hear one kid super pissed going - *Yo mama is so fat, it took me two buses and a train to get to her good side.* The other boy threw his plate at him and said ''*My momma is thin you fu*k*'' I swear, I almost choked on my water.

Extra virgin olive oil – Virgin… Remember these days when dinosaurs roamed the earth. Yes, that is how long ago it went out for you.

Kosher salt – All hail the OG of the kitchen. Salt.

Black pepper – I got hit in the head with a can of Dr. Pepper today. Luckily I'm not hurt, it was a soft drink

½ red onion - I always loved red onion more. I swear, she makes you *cry X10 more!*

5 garlic cloves – If you add to much, you might not get none tonight. Stinky!

½ teaspoon red pepper flakes (or 1 teaspoon Aleppo pepper flakes) – Spicy, that used to be your love life. I will leave it at that! Do not look at me… Look at your spouse!

1 teaspoon dry oregano – Up there I said your love life was spicy! Well now its dry like this ingredient!

1 cup dry white wine – If you have any wine left at home (you alcoholic) I usually use Pinot-Grigio.

1 lemon zested and juiced – If you do not know how to zest a damn lemon then please whip out your smart phone and repeat after me. ''HOW TO ZEST A LEMON''. If she cannot help you neither can I.

Parmesan cheese to your liking – Who does not love this stinky chunk… Do not say it out loud your spouse might look over.

Large handful chopped fresh parsley about 1 cup packed – Fresh, none of that dry crap. Your sex life is already so dry and depressing switch to natural fresh ingredients.

2 to 3 vine ripe tomatoes chopped. – Chop these fuc*ers up!

Pg.15

Do This:

FIRST, thank you for trusting me with your Mediterranean dream! First, cook the pasta in salted boiling water according to package (about 9-10minutes). Reserve a little bit of the starchy pasta cooking water. Drain the pasta well. Thank you. Moving on!

MEANWHILE our hot lovely pasta is cooking, cook the shrimp. Whip out a large pan heat 1 tablespoon extra-virgin olive oil over medium-high heat until the oil is shimmering but not smoking. *No smoking!* Cook the shrimp on each side for 2 to 3 minutes until it turns pink. Transfer the shrimp to a side plate for now. Are you excited? You better be!

IN THE same pan add a little more extra virgin olive oil, if needed of course. Reduce the heat to medium-low. Now please add onions, garlic, oregano and red pepper flakes. Cook for 2 to 3 minutes, stirring constantly. *Now best part to all my alcohol lovers* - Add wine to the pan and scrape up any pieces of garlic and onions. Cook the wine for 1 minute to reduce then add the lemon juice and lemon zest. *YUMMY!*

ADD THE chopped parsley and tomatoes, toss about for about 30 to 40 seconds. Season with Kosher salt. *Do not over salt it!*

NOW MY LOVE! Add cooked pasta to the pan and toss to coat. Add some of the pasta starchy water if you need to.

FINALLY, I know you waited forever for this! Now add the cooked shrimp. Allow the shrimp to warm through briefly *(another 30 seconds)*, then remove the pasta from heat.

TO FINISH, sprinkle a little (or a lot) grated parmesan cheese and more red pepper flake. Serve immediately!

***Disclaimer:** Please be careful not to burn your finger. Also, get yourself a glass of wine you deserve it! You made it! Proud of you. If you fuc*ed it up – well, try again! K bye. *

What will you pour into the shot glass after cooking?

- [ ] ALCOHOL DUH! I deserve it after sweating my a*s of in the kitchen.
- [ ] WATER, I am whack like that.

ZITTI WITTYY MEATBALLS!

Yummy! Cheesy! Amazing!

About the dish:

Hello there my lovely chefs! If this is your first recipe you went for then YES! Good choice! Welcome to my balls! Meatballs! I mean… WOW ok moving on… Baked ziti meatballs. It is originally an Italian recipe *(at least that is what daddy internet tells us.)* Well, it is my own magical special super-duper twist *(too much I know I get that a lot).* This is my tweaked recipe, and it is tasty. At least I think that. No casualties yet after this! So far so good! It is an Italian dish… and what is more Italian than WINE! Get a glass! *(One for me too! Share damn!).* Well, this came from throwing things into a bowl and voila something good came out of this. I am telling you everyone loves my balls! Meatballs! Get your mind out of gutter! *MOVING ON!* You will not regret trying this! It works for parties or just you. Okay, love you bye.

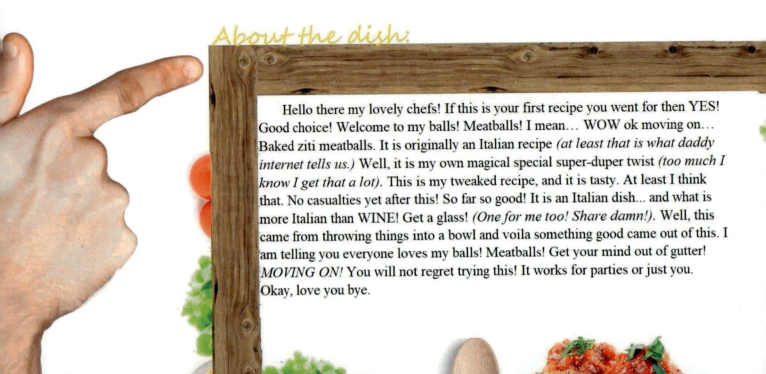

Serving: Around 10! WOW I know. Leftovers are calling your name!

Prep time: 15 minutes.

Cook time: 30 minutes all together. At least that is what I think. Who am I to talk though? Oh yeah, the author. I forgot. *Listen to me!*

Get This:

1 1/2 Package of ziti pasta - You know every supermarket has it! Stop being lazy get up and get going!

1 onion chopped - My friend goes: My wallet is like an onion, whenever I open it I cry. Totally can relate!

4 Gloves of garlic - You can never go wrong with garlic... Unless you want to kiss after then no.... a hard pass!

1 cup of fresh chopped parsley - I love parsley... It is clear I add a lot of it to everything. #DadJokeOfTheDay ... What is green and can sing? ELVIS PARSLEY! .. Please do not leave....

1-pound lean ground beef - You can use chicken or turkey instead as well. And if you are vegan this recipe is not for you. I am sorry. There are salads you can try though!

2 (26 ounce) jars marinara sauce – This is how Italians use a like button!

1 cup of breadcrumbs - Any breadcrumbs, flavored... not flavored (kind of like your love life sadly).

1 teaspoon of pepper & salt. - My friend asked her husband: "What do you like the most in me: my pretty face or my sexy body?" He looked at her from head to toe and replied: "I like your sense of humor." I never laughed so much!

1 Egg - My friends son told me this: *I said to my teacher*, "I don't think I deserved zero for this exam. *She said*, "I agree, but I couldn't give you any less." I did not know what to say! Sorry kiddo!

2 TBS of oregano – What herb never says yes? oregaNO! Wow, I am so lame I am sorry!

2 cups of ricotta cheese - My dad loves to eat. My mom goes: You eat so much that your favourite necklace is the food chain. Oyy....

2 1/2 cups of mozzarella – Had a long day? Take a damn shot!

1 1/2 cup grated Parmesan cheese - Do not hesitate with that shot. Your day was long enough. You had earned it! Bottoms up! NOT YOU SEAN SIT DOWN. Not that kind of bottom!

Pg.19

Do This.

BRING a large pot of lightly salted water to a boil. Add ziti pasta and cook until al dente (uhm look at him he is bilingual), about 8 minutes; drain. *Kind of like you drain your day at work. Slow and sloppy*

IN A BOWL, throw in that nice beef in. Chop onion into small pieces (here is a tissue for those tears!) then also dump it into the bowl. Add pepper, salt, half cup of chopped parsley (leave the other half for later) add 2 gloves of minced garlic, 1 egg & 1TBS of oregano. Now mix it all. Now take breadcrumbs and 1 cup of parmesan cheese and mix again! Now shape meatballs out of that. (For the shape-not-understanding specimens that is round...)

TAKE out a pan, throw in some oil. Add your meatballs on it. Cook on medium for about 4-5 minutes each side (if your balls are small... well this did not sound good... Well, if they are small, it might take less than 5 minutes each side*Insert a joke*.) Once cooked set aside.

NOW take out a decent size pot add all marinara sauce to it along with 2 gloves of garlic minced. Now add remaining parsley and 2 cups of ricotta cheese. MIX on a medium heat. Boil for only 5 minutes.

BUTTER a 9x13 inch (WOW) baking dish, baking dish LINDA! Get your head out of the gutter. Lay out your balls first, then add some sauce in between finish with 1 cup of mozzarella cheese. On top of that add ziti, then add remaining sauce and add remaining cheeses along with oregano! Preheat the oven to 350 degrees F. Leave it inside for 10 minutes (as your meatballs should be mostly cooked already). Take out, you are done! Enjoy! Pairs well with champagne, surprisingly.

*Disclaimer: Like I said it pairs well with champagne... At least it paired well that one night in Rome.... That is what I call my couch. But do not trust me on that. I have terrible taste in liquor. Seriously. Ask my friends. *

[1] **PICK ONE** [2]

I deserve a shot. I nailed this recipe.   I screwed up.
                                            I get nothing.

Cajun Bacon Madness Pasta!

(Eat at your own risk, its spicy as hell. At least to me but I am weak when it comes to spicy food so maybe I am a bad example).

About the dish:

This recipe is an ancient Greek recipe. Came from no other place than all mighty Athens... Of course, this is a total Bu*l - Sh*it. Unless my kitchen is Greece and Athens is my fridge. However, I got cha! I thought it would sound more interesting. Since I have your attention now, I am sad to disappoint you that this is just a recipe I came out with today! Today was somewhere in 2021. It is little spicy but good! I mean I am probably not fitted to judge how spicy food is as everything is spicy to me… Let me put it this way… Mild to me is like Habanero spicy for you. I know I am lame. At least I do not hide it! Give this pasta a go! I know you say ''David another pasta, blah blah blah can you cook anything else...'' First, OUCH! Second fully F-U.., Thriftly YES THERE IS MORE THAN PASTA IN THIS BOOK! Just wait! Moving on!

Serving: 4 Humans, 1 alien, 4 dogs and absolutely no cats.

Prep time: 10 minutes. Perhaps... IDK how quick you are.

Cook time: 25 minutes.

Get This.

2 Large chicken breasts - Make sure that they are large. No flappy ones please. This is not chicken fashion week. This is Fat Sunday!

2 Cups of fried crushed bacon – You must fry it before! Yummy! Who does not love beacon? Looking at my vegans moving grass.... *Please do not murder me* This is just a joke. Forgive me.

1 cup of milk - For the bones! At least that is what daddy Internet says! #DadJokeOfTheDay ... Where do cow astronauts stop to get a drink? ... MILKYWAY! *You are not laughing* I know, I am terrible at jokes. What a confidence boost. Cancel me!

1 cup of chicken broth - #AnotherDadJokeOfTheDay - What do you get when you cross a chicken with a bell? *An alarm cluck.*

1 TBS - Of... Cajun spice, black pepper, red paprika spice & garlic powder. (I did not feel like listing it all one by one. So, cluster it is!) Do not mix. Just have separate spoons or whatever.

2 TBS spoons of sour cream - Sour like your soul.

1 Teaspoon of salt & red pepper flakes. - DO NOT MIX. Seriously though. Listen to me for once in your life!

1 cup of breadcrumbs - You can either use plain, or flavored ones. Who cares... not me!

1/2 cup of all-purpose flour also

2 spoons of flour for the sauce!

1 penne pasta box. - Make sure to get bigger penne...

2 TBS of virgin olive oil. – You wish you were one!

Do This:

TAKE your breast *(chicken breast)* and cut into small pieces *(little bigger than a quarter)* chop, chop all of them and place into a large bowl. Now add pepper, paprika, garlic powder, salt & oil. Mix it together. Once you had mixed these ingredients, add breadcrumbs and 1/2 cup of flour. MIX again!

YOU are making a fuc*ing mess. Slow down! Once done, set aside for 15 minutes until the flavors bond. *We are sad to inform that this does not work on humans. Your flavors will not bond if you set yourself aside for 15 minutes rolled in this* That sh*t expired already. Unsalvageable.

MEANWHILE Let us play TIC TAC TOE! To kill some time!

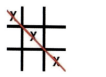 *Joke, I already won. Stop Trying.*

NOW take a pot and add some salt and boil penne. After this dreadful long waiting time passes. You can kill it by taking a sip of champagne. Do not worry who will judge you? The onion your cutting?... Take out a pan, add some oil and place chicken on it. Lave on medium. Let it fry. Meanwhile, take out a small/medium pot. Add 2 spoons of flour, Cajun spice, red pepper flakes, sour cream, milk and chicken stock. Mix it before you put the heat on. **Make sure** flour combines well with all the liquid. Now set it on medium/high. Stir until your sauce gets thicker. Once it does. Set aside.

GOING back to the pan, flip the chicken on the other side. Let it fry. Once it is almost done chop onion into slices, add to the chicken. Once onion & chicken is done cooking, add already fried crushed bacon & stir it all baby! Make sure chicken cooked through. Once it is done set aside. Get a big bowl, add cooked penne, add chicken & sauce. Mix it well. Now eat! Enjoy its bit spicy though! Garnish with scallion or as some people call it green onions.

***Disclaimer**: May cause a spicy visit in the restroom. I say screw it, get some mimosas ready! *

Ask someone who pisses you off or upsets you - to turn this book upside down - the message on the side reveals itself to the reader.

1041 2406 29

Pg. 23

Dijon Pork Chopsies!
For the pork lovers!

About the dish:

Hello there, my lovely little chefs! I thought we finally have a switch from shrimp and chicken, and we go onto pork now! I present to you Dijon pork chopsies! This recipe is half inspired half nailed! Pork Chops with Mushrooms and Shallots are so juicy and flavorful, made with a creamy homemade Dijon sauce perfect for weeknight dinners, weeknight drinking games *(who said that)*, hangover in general - it is a great recipe. You will not regret this decision! Check out our sides in this book! Some pair super well with this! OK, get your cute self-cooking! Get yourself a cold beer or water with lemon. Whatever you want – I am not judging you this time. *OKAY GO!*

Serving: 4 adult human beings, 2 dogs, 1 cat.

Prep time: 10 minutes if you know what you are doing son!

Cook time: 25 minutes! Stop complaining.

Get This:

1 tsp butter or ghee – I once asked my friend's kid how old his grandpa is. He replied: *So old that he used to ride a dinosaur to school.* Ouch!

Black pepper – This is unrelated but hear me out. My grandpa is a jokester, and he goes! *What kind of shoes does your grandma like?* I said: *What kind?* He says: *Grandma prefers slip-on shoes.* Me: *Why?* Him: *It is easier for her to throw it at me.* Should I be concerned?

4 pork loin chops, bone-in, trimmed or 1 lb. (boneless) - I know what a shocker I am using something different than chicken and shrimp! Shocker! I am as shocked as you. I am not Basic like your EX-honey!

1/4 cup chopped shallots - #DadJokeOfTheDay - *I LOVE YOU SHALLOT!* ... Lame joke of the day. If this even qualifies as a joke. Listen I am trying. It is late, I am tired give me some credit. I am really trying to introduce your basic heart to amazing cuisine. So shut up. K bye.

10 oz sliced baby Bella mushrooms - Or just whatever mushrooms you find at your local store. Just wanted it to sound fancy. Bella! It is like we are in Italy... But this is not Italy, and you are no BELLA! JOKE!

1/2 tsp kosher salt - Salty, over here.

1 cup low sodium chicken stock – or broth ... Once my friends kid got detention. According to him this is what happened. <u>HIS OLDER TEACHER:</u> "If I say, 'I am beautiful,' which tense is that?" <u>HE REPLIED:</u> "It is obviously past."... Poor kid was just honest.

1 tbsp Dijon mustard - Make sure it is DIJON. #Fun FACT! My favorite singer is *Celine DIJON*.. *Awkward laugh* Okay I am leaving!

2 tbsp chopped fresh parsley - I am telling you, fresh is always best. Unlike your style. Not so fresh. Not so good. Kind of plain. Funny story: My friend and his wife always roast each other. The other day this happened. He goes: *Your butt is so big it has it's own zip code.* She did not wait long and replied: *You are so fat not even Dora could explore you.* Surprisingly, they had been married for 10 years!

Do This:

IN A large frying pan heat the butter over moderately low heat. Season them lovely chops with salt and pepper. Raise heat to medium *(kind of like when hubby pisses you off and your heat rises)* and add the chops to the pan and sauté for 7 minutes. Longer if needed.

TURN, turn and turn until chops are browned and done to medium (kind of like you after a bad visit at a tanning salon), about 7-8 minutes longer or until the pork reads 160F in the center. If you do not have a thermometer... Then just nail it LINDA! Remove the chops and put in a warm spot once done. Almost halfway done! *(If you do not have a thermometer cut one chop in half and check if inside is cooked through).*

ADD shallots to the pan and cook, stirring, until soft, about 3-4 minutes. Or longer if needed!

ADD the stock to deglaze the pan, stir in the mustard, 1 tbsp parsley, then add mushrooms, season with fresh pepper and cook about 3-5 minutes, or until mushrooms are done. *Do not BURN IT!*

PLACE the chops on a platter and pour the mushroom sauce over the meat, make it drip! Top with remaining parsley.

QUCIK MASH POTATOES:

4 Large potatoes any kind, peel, cut in small pieces boil until cooked! Now drain water, add *4TBS of milk, 2 TBS of butter, ½ cup of cream* cheese now MASH! Add some *salt and pepper* for taste! Cut about *½ cup of fresh parsley* add to the mash potatoes.

If you want real kick add *crushed bacon*! You are welcome! You can also pair with other sides from this book. Go to table of content – *SIDES!*

QUICK FRIES:

Get *4 large potatoes*. Peel them. Slice the potatoes into ½ inch thick sticks. Using a French fry cutter makes this much easier. Heat oil in a pan so that fries can submerge. Cook until golden on medium heat. Take out & place in a non-plastic bowl, cut some *fresh parsley* and *mince some garlic*. Mix it all in a bowl with some salt and pepper to taste. *VOILA!*

Disclaimer: Don't overcook the chopsies! Pairs well with wine! That is all, bye. Now go get fat and sassy!

CRISPY CHIPOTLE HONEY Chick'n
Kind of hot like you.

About the dish:

Okay real question here! *Who does not like crispy chicken!?* Oh my, oh my! This mouthwatering delicious chick'n will rock your little stomach. Originated in Chicago on diver's street… For those who live in Chicago -Yeah ok, no it is not from Chicago and such street does not exist. For rest of you ignore this. This recipe is inspired by all of you. *Kind of hot kind of spicy people.* You are welcome. Delicious flavor of both chili and honey makes this dish into a superb, delicious dinner. *It is quick, easy!* Pairs well with fries and side salad! Do not worry you do not need to search through the book to find fries recipe. I included a quick garlic and parsley fries at the bottom of this recipe as well as quick salad. You're welcome. I also did not want you to ruin pages with your dirty fingers searching in the end! *Again, you are welcome.* So thoughtful. Also, Sorry for making this recipe quite long. I've got some good stories to tell!

Serving: About damn 4 I would say! Maybe 5?

Prep time: 15 minutes. Kind of.

Cook time: 30 Minutes! Okay, so I am kind of rounding this up. I might have screwed up the time. Let us say 25-30 minutes.

OKAY SO THIS ONE IS TAD LONGER RECIPE SO IT IS ON MORE THAN ONE PAGE! I AM SORRY I AM TRYING TO MAKE THIS EASY.

Get This:

12 chicken tenderloins - Them thick ones!

6-8 cups Canola oil or shortening - Or whatever you got.

FOR THE BATTER

1 egg – My grandpa goes! *You know what's the difference between eggs, and you? Eggs get laid, you do not.* Ops he did it again! What a savage!

1/4 teaspoon pepper - #DadJokeOfTheDay - What do you call a spice with a PHD... a Dr. Pepper.

1/4 teaspoon garlic powder - My momma always said that garlic powder makes everything better so when I was young, I sprinkled some on my parents' marriage certificate... you guessed they divorced. I Fuc*ed up!

1/2 cup milk – Santa once asked me: *What do you want for Christmas?* Me: *You want to know what I want for Christmas? My dad to come back with the milk he said he was going to get...*

1 1/4 teaspoons salt - Funny story, once I went over my best friend's girlfriends house for a family dinner. You know whole family and such... His GF said, " *Daddy please pass me the salt.*" then he and her dad grabbed salt... Awkward. He knows!

3/4 cup flour - Sniffany no!

1/2 cup chicken broth - #AnotherDadJokeOfTheDay - What animal gets easily offended? The chicken: they always get roasted. Sadly!

CONTINUE TO NEXT PAGE

FOR THE BREADING

2 teaspoons of paprika - Funny story time... Once I was talking to my teacher about whales. The teacher said it was physically impossible for a whale to swallow a human because it was an exceptionally large mammal, however its throat is ridiculously small. I stated that Jonah was swallowed by a whale. Irritated, the teacher reiterated that a whale could not swallow a human; it was physically impossible. Then I said... *"When I get to Heaven, I will ask Jonah. "*. The teacher asked, *"What if Jonah went to Hell?"* Me pissed off -, *"Then you ask him."* I got an F.

1 1/2 cups flour - Since we are on story lines. Once I was at a restaurant next to me were two kids... One kid said...Yo mama so dumb she got hit by a cup and told the police she got mugged. I almost choked on my bagel.

1 teaspoon black pepper - My French friend said this once.... It is embarrassing when you go over someone's house and there is no PEPPER... I am like: *I don't get it*... he goes. *Have you ever used bathroom with no PEPPER!* That is how I learned my friend Pierre says PAPER, but it sounds like pepper.

1 teaspoon garlic powder - Let us take a break! These stories were long! This recipe became ridiculously long! But good material though!

1 teaspoon salt - #AnotherDadJokeOfTheDay -Why is the sea salty? Because the land never waves back....

FOR THE HONEY CHIPOTLE SAUCE

1/4 cup water - You might need more than a cup after last night you party animal.

1/4 cup ketchup – Fun-Fact! According to recent science research they said tomatoes are "fruit" does that mean ketchup is a smoothie. I am baffled!

2/3 cup honey - Remember the day when you first met your loved one and they called you honey all the time... now it is just flat out... Bi*ch. Times change.

1-2 teaspoons chipotle chili powder - #AnotherDadJokeOfTheDay... What do you call a cow in the snow? Chili Beef...

1 tablespoon apple cider vinegar - My grandpa goes... *Do you know what vinegar and Aunt Gina have in common?* I am like ...what? He goes... *They are both bitter as f*ck.*

1/2 teaspoon hot sauce - So my grandma is really a savage as well... She told me once... If your boyfriend ever pisses you off... put some hot sauce on your lips... And then you know... go down. I wonder what else they used to teach kids in 1955!

1/2 teaspoon salt - My grandma to my grandpa: *You're so old that when you had science class the only elements on the periodic table were earth, wind, water and fire.* He goes: *Aren't you my age!* He got her!

*Disclaimer: This might get you addicted. Also, no jokes are meant to harm anyone. It is just for sh*t and giggles people.*

Do This:

GET your small sauce pan out, combine honey, ketchup, water, vinegar, salt, chili powder, and hot sauce. Bring that bi*ch to simmer and cook for 2 minutes, stirring frequently. After remove from heat.

BATTER: In a medium bowl whisk together milk, egg, chicken broth, pepper, salt, and garlic powder. Whisk in flour. Make sure it all combines well!

BREADING: Combine all ingredients for breading in a bowl mix well. Do something right!

HEAT oil in a pot to 350-355F (for deep frying). Dip chicken in batter and then roll to coat in breading. Then Fry 4 at a time, frying until golden brown and cooked through, about 4-6 minutes. Place cooked chicken tenderloins in a large bowl and toss with honey chipotle sauce you had made. Voila! You are welcome!

QUICK FRIES:

Get 4 large potatoes. Peel them. Slice the potatoes into ½ inch thick sticks. Using a French fry cutter makes this much easier. Heat oil in a pan so that fries can submerge. Cook until golden on medium heat. Take out & place in a non-plastic bowl, cut some fresh parsley and mince some garlic. Mix it all in a bowl with some salt and pepper to taste. *VOILA!*

QUICK SIDE SALAD:

Cut some *lettuce* into a bowl, cut *1 tomatoe, half cucumber, 1 onion* and *1 cup of corn*. Afterwards, add *2 cups shredded cheese,* then mix ½ *cup of sour cream* with ½ *cup of salsa*. Mix all well. If you do not have salsa. Ditch the sour cream and salsa and dump whatever dressing you have in your fridge!

☐ PICK ONE ☐

I deserve a shot. If you are underage - get outta here.   *I deserve nothing.*

OPA Chicken Gyro
For the Greek lovers!

About the dish:

Close your eyes and imagine Mediterranean Sea! You say *OH NO DAVID NOT AGAIN WITH THIS!* Sh*t just trust me!... If you have crappy imagination sniff on some basil turn a fan on should help! I know, I know your trailer, apartment or home is no Greece! *Moving on, I personally love Greece!* Food, History! UGH, gorgeous beaches and so on! Well, who does not know about a gyro? Originally, made with lamb however, I know you will probably prefer chicken! This recipe also has its homemade tzatziki sauce! *YOU ARE WELCOME!* Cook time is quick so if you prepare marinade day before your dish should take no longer than 20 minutes! So, take some plates break them and shout fuc*ing *OPA!* Watch your husband or wife thinking you lost your sh*t finally! It is what it is!

Serving: Sort of 6-7 maybe can push it to 8.

Prep Time: 2 hours and 30 minutes. It is long because of MARINADE!

Cook Time: 15 minutes! Perhaps.

Get This:

2 pounds chicken tenderloins - What day do chickens hate most? Fry-day! But this is not the day! Moving on.

1 1/2 tablespoons olive oil - Preferable olive oil. However, if you are on budget and have only basic oil... Use it, I mean you might just give yourself visit in the bathroom. In case STOCK up on paper like it is Coronavirus. I am obviously just joking.

1 tablespoon freshly squeezed lemon juice - Fresh, you used to be fresh... What happened.

3 cloves garlic minced - The best kiss killer in the world! Next time instead of faking stomachache or headache in bed eat garlic. Your loved one will pass! If you know what I mean.

2 teaspoons dried oregano - #DadJokeOfTheDay - Why did the chef add extra oregano to the sauce? He was making up for lost thyme. Thank you, thank you. I will just show myself out now.

1 teaspoon dried thyme - Dried, reminds me a lot of your life. Dried out...

1/2 teaspoon paprika - For the non-mathematical specimens that is half of a teaspoon.

6-8 pita flatbreads - Funny story I was once at a playground with my little nephew... And I hear these kids arguing... One goes ... Your momma so flat she looks like a flatbread. This is the day I learned that kids are savage AF. For real!

2 cups shredded romaine - #AnotherDadJokeOfTheDay - What do you get when you throw lettuce into the ocean? I do not know lettuce sea. Please do not fuc*ing cancel me!

2 cups cherry tomatoes quartered - If you do not have cherry tomatoes. Any tomatoes would do.

1 red onion thinly sliced - My friend has an amazing marriage. They continuously roast each other. The other day his wife said to him: *I am not saying that you are stupid, just that you are constantly unlucky when you try thinking.* His response was quick: *The IQ chart doesn't go below 75. You can stop trying to go lower Rebecca.*

Ingredients for tzaziki sauce. Next page!

FOR THE TZATZIKI SAUCE

3/4 cup Greek yogurt - Any brand really.

1/2 cup grated English cucumber, squeezed dry - You know a lot about dry, therefore this step should not be hard. Use your dry sex life as reference. Never seen anything drier.

2 tablespoons chopped fresh dill - When I was a toddler, my parents would always say, "Excuse my French" just after a swear word. I'll never forget the first day at school when my teacher asked if any of us knew any French. I thought I was fluent until I recieved an F and call to parents.

2 tablespoons freshly squeezed lemon juice - FRESH LEMONS! Make sure you get the seeds out. Do not choke anyone! STOP LOOKING AT YOUR MOTHER IN LAW.

2 teaspoons lemon zest - If you do not know what this is or how to do this... look it up online. They do not pay me enough.

1 clove garlic, minced - Who does not love garlic? Seriously. VAMPIRES!

Kosher salt and freshly ground black pepper, to taste - My friend's wife is a savage. She wanted to talk him into braces and said: *You have so many gaps in your teeth it looks like your tongue is in jail.* Of course, he did not wait long enough and clapped back saying: *You're ass so big that when you fell over no one was laughing but the ground sure was cracking up.* She then replied: *When you look in the mirror, say hi to the clown you see in there for me, would ya?* Then he replied: *You just might be why the middle finger was invented in the first place.* They had been married for a long time! Guess, recipe for lasting relationship is this? Who knows.

Chug one you need it!

Onto the next page!

Pg.33

Do This:

HOW TO MAKE TZAZIKI SAUCE: Combine Greek yogurt, cucumber, dill, lemon juice, lemon zest and garlic; season with salt and pepper, to desired taste. Set aside in the refrigerator for at least 15 minutes to set.

TIP FOR MORE FLAVORED CHICKEN: Take a fork and make holes in the tenderloins. That way marinade can get inside.

GET a gallon size zip lock bag *(if you do not have one throw it in the pot then)*, combine olive oil, chicken, lemon juice, garlic, thyme, oregano, paprika, 1/2 teaspoon and 1 teaspoon salt pepper. Mix it, if you are using the bag shake it around so chicken gets covered with marinade. Marinate for at least 2 and half hours. Drain the chicken from the marinade if using a grill if not continue reading.

PREHEAT grill to medium heat *(If you do not own one, use a skillet do not discard marinade use it for cooking)*. Add chicken to grill, and cook, turning occasionally, until chicken is completely cooked through, reaching an internal temperature of 165 degrees F, about 8 minutes. If you are using a skillet, Cook tenderloins about 4-5 minutes on each side in marinade.

TO SERVE, warm pitas on the grill, about 1-2 minutes per side. Halve pitas, and fill with chicken, romaine lettuce, tomatoes, red onion and tzatziki sauce. If you do not own a damn grill, use a microwave or a toaster. **DO NOT MAKE THE PITA HARD** as it will be hard to fold it. Tastes great with fries inside. To make quick fries get two large potatoes, cut into stick, fry on oil until golden brown. Season with pepper and salt to taste.! **ENJOY!**

Serve immediately.

*Disclaimer: The longer you hold the sauce in the fridge the better it is. Also, get a damn grill! About time to adult. *

QUICK FRIES:

Get *4 large potatoes*. Peel them. Slice the potatoes into ½ inch thick sticks. Using a French fry cutter makes this much easier. Heat oil in a pan so that fries can submerge. Cook until golden on medium heat. Take out & place in a non-plastic bowl. Add salt and pepper to taste. VOILA!

Challenge Only for 21+

☐ 1 shot of vodka   ☐ 1 shot of hot sauce

Though I will let you off so easy?
SIKE

Loaded Stuffed Shells
Super yummy, super easy!

About the dish:

Who does not love marinara sauce, cheese and other cr*p from this recipe? We all do... I mean even if you are on diet... Cheesy shells sound good right now? Oh, damn did I just pushed you to cheat on your diet? Whoops... Anyways, stuffed shells are a popular dish for good a reason... *Reason #1* They are good... *Reason #2* Easy to make... *Reason #3* Not many ingredients involved. Therefore, if you are lazy today and do not want to think... Just nail this recipe. Even if you have two left hands and cannot cook for sh*t ... I doubt you would have problem with this one. If you do. You might want to write a cra*py review to your parents regarding how they made you!... Well, if you are not a cook, you might find this recipe thrilling and super simple. Go, I believe in you

Pg.35

Get This:

Servings: 6 unless you are Shamu the whale like me than maybe 2!

Prep Time: 25 minutes... Unless you are clumsy, and sh*t then add extra time for cleanup.

Cook Time: 30 minutes!

24 jumbo pasta shells cooked according to package directions - Make sure you follow the damn package directions though. Some brands take longer. Some less longer, kind of like you. If you know what I mean.

15 ounces ricotta cheese - #DadJokeOfTheDay ... What did one cheese say to the other during philosophy class? "I dis a brie." *Please do not cancel me! *

3 cups shredded mozzarella cheese - (divided use) - Okay, follow me on this one. It is a brain game! What do you get by mixing Mozart and Cinderella together? Any guesses? C'mon Trudy! *MOZART+CINDERELLA= MOZARELLA!* *Walks out of the room*

1/2 cup grated parmesan cheese - Okay not another cheese joke! Oh, my cheesus!

2 teaspoons dry Italian seasoning - Funny story, my friend's Italian grandma Allegra once asked me a question... which went... *David what does my husband and dried package spice have in common?* So, I go... - *What?* Then she replies ... *They are both dry as fu*k..* I almost swallowed my spoon. Let me add that we all were eating dinner together. She has some jokes!

1 large egg - I once said. Eggs get laid - you do not.

2 TBS parsley chopped - While chopping make sure you don't chop your fuc*ing finger.

2 TBS of basil - #AnotherDadJokeOfTheDay - Buckle up your seatbelts! Okay, so basil wanted to meet with sage, but it was getting late. He decided to ask oregano, "what THYME is it?" Thyme gets it! ha-ha, no? Okay... Well, Sh*t.

3 cups marinara sauce divided use - Okay, totally unrelated... My neighbor goes... *The human rectum can stretch up to 9 inches without tearing. A raccoon can fit through holes that are 6 inches or wider. So technically you can fit an entire racoon up your arse!* ... Okay... Thanks Frida for the information... Never looked at her the same again since.

Cooking spray - For the non-educated specimens... Cooking spray is ... an oil in spray. An Oil you can spray out of the bottle. Thank you for attention. Goodbye. Adios! Cia! Ciao!

Do This:

Disclaimer: If your husband/wife is still being a jerk switch his marinara sauce with a hot sauce. Thank me later. Also, not responsible for any moral OR physical damages caused! K Bye onto the next one! *

Disclaimer: Cook shells prior! Acoording to package.

PREHEAT your oven to 380 degrees F. Buy a 9"x13" baking pan ... Or if you already have it - spray it with cooking spray. Less is more for the crazy sprayers out there.

SPREAD 1 1/2 cups of the marinara sauce in an even layer in the bottom of the pan. Get a bowl! Now place that lovely ricotta cheese, 1 1/2 cups of mozzarella cheese, Italian seasoning, basil, egg, salt, pepper and parmesan cheese in that bowl. Stir to combine.

NOW... Fill each shell with the ricotta mixture and place in the baking dish. Layer remaining marinara sauce over the shells, sprinkle the other 1 1/2 cups of cheese over the top. Take a deep shot. You deserve it. If your husband or wife is complaining... Tell them to shut the hell up.

COVER the dish with foil. Bake for 20 minutes. Then uncover the pan, bake for an additional 10 minutes or until cheese is melted and starting to brown. If you want more cheese... I usually do... Dump some more on top.

Sprinkle with parsley, serve!

Now a crossword!

Down
1. Word that describes your BOSS.
2. An alcoholic drink made from fermented grape juice.
4. An alcoholic drink made from yeast-fermented malt.
5. an alcoholic drink
6. legal drinking age in the USA.
7. Don't do this if you are drunk
10. When your spouse pisses you off he/she is a ?

Across
3. _____ Bahamas.
8. Skip 8. This makes no sense just like your choices sometimes.
9. After a long day you need more _____?

Grand Imperium Lasagna
Cheesy and beautiful like you!

About the dish:

Who does not love lasagna?! Especially super cheesy one! This dish originated in Naples, Italy in Middle Ages at least that is what daddy interned told me. He is usually right. Unless I clicked on the wrong link. Anyways, I just served you with some great valuable information that you can use in your next conversation. *Kind of rhymes!* This is my little twist to the traditional lasagna. It is easy, delicious and cheesy like you. This dish does not require any special cooking skills. Yes, I am looking at you. I see you but we are missing skills. However, do not sh*t a brick Becky! This easy recipe is just for you! Pair with any booze of choice-you are all set!

Serving: 12 human beings, one cow (your mother-in-law?) – unless she is nice then you are lucky!

Prep Time: 30 minutes – unless you spill something you clumsy goof!

Cook Time: 1 hour – relax it isn't that long!

Get This:

½ pound lean ground beef, chicken or turkey. - Any of these 3 magnificent choices will do. I sometimes mix all. No side effects yet. *Waves at you with 3rd arm* - ops!

5 cups mozzarella cheese shredded - The more cheese the better. Don't you agree?

12 lasagna noodles uncooked - Wife to husband: You're so big, your belt size is an "equator."

2 cups of parmesan cheese - Parmesan smells like socks... Maybe it is just me.

½ pound Italian sausage – Fun fact from my friend Marco! Prepare! This was his school project.

1 onion diced – Another Fun Fact - What can you make from onion and beans? A tear GAS! Or your uncle Giuseppe fart.

2 cloves garlic minced - The beautiful breath killer...

36 ounces pasta sauce - Any choice! Of course, red... any flavor. *Marinara works best for me!*

2 tablespoons tomato paste - #DadJokeOfTheDay - At a restaurant called Apathy, they only give you a spoon to eat your food with......when I told the owner it was hard to eat my spaghetti he said, "Well... I don't give a fork."

1 teaspoon Italian seasoning - I switched all the labels on my mom's spice rack.... I'm not in trouble yet but the *thyme is cumin*. Mic drops!

2 cups ricotta cheese - My friend's kid is something else. His dad is short. He goes: Dad is so short, he went to see Santa and he told him to get back to work.

¼ cup fresh parsley chopped - My friend's grandpa about his wife: Lauren is so old she owes moses a dollar.

1 egg beaten - Ouch. Your husband just ran for his life!

Do This:

HEAT oven to 350°F. Cook pasta al dente *Oh he sounds international* according to package directions. Rinse under cold water and set aside. Fun tip! ... I honestly do not have any. Fry beef (or other victim you chose), sausage, onion and garlic over medium high heat until no pink remains. Drain any fart. I mean FAT!

STIR in pasta sauce, tomato paste, Italian seasoning. Simmer 5 minutes. *Laugh like a witch so people think you are crazy. Live a little.

MAKE Cheese Mixture by combining 1 ½ cups mozzarella, ¼ cup parmesan cheese, ricotta, parsley, and egg. MIX, Mix, Mix! Add 1 cup meat sauce to a 9x13 pan. Usually, the size of an average... New York apartment you dirty minded human. Top with 3 lasagna noodles. Layer with ⅓ of the Cheese Mixture and 1 cup of meat sauce. Repeat twice more.

FINISH with 3 noodles topped with remaining sauce. Cover with foil and bake for 45 minutes. Uncover, sprinkle with remaining cheese (2 ½ cups mozzarella cheese and ¼ cup parmesan) and bake an additional 15 minutes or until browned and bubbly. Broil 2-3 minutes if desired. Sprinkle some basil and fresh parsley on top.

REST 10-15 minutes before cutting. ENJOY this magnificent dish. Now grab a beer.

Disclaimer: No Italians were harmed while creating this recipe. Also, this is all humor do not get offended. Do not ask for manager. I ain't got one

PICK ONE CARD!

| TAKE A SHOT IF YOU ARE TIRED OF BS Any liqour. If you are under the age of 21 get the hell out of this game. Your time will come! | SING YOUR FAVORITE SONG! Sing your heart out. LOUD! No cheating! | THIS WAS A CRAPPY DAY I DESERVE A ROMANTIC DINNER Show this to your husband, wife, gf, bf or whoever or whatever you are dating. TIP: Close your eyes, open the book, choose a random page. VOILA your romantic dinner! |

Fried Chick'n ! Fingerlicious!
Kind of like you! Okay, buy me a dinner first.

About the dish:

Let me ask you this, *who on earth does not like fried chicken?!?* Even if you are a fit athlete or run your a*s on the treadmill daily, you still would grab that greasy chick'n on your cheat day! Well, if you like that crispy chick'n vibe - then this is for you. If you are a *SHAMU WHALE* like me... It is a perfect SNACK! Ha-ha-ha ... No but really do not judge me. This specially kicks in good after a night out *(if you have some left!)* - so make sure you do it before your long night at the nightclub. You will love eating this after getting home without one shoe and messed up hair. This pairs well with anything really! If you want less calories... *Eat a damn ice cube*. K bye! Dish inspired by no other than the state of Louisiana!

Pg.41

Serving: 5 If you know how to share.
Prep time: 15 mins.
Cook time: All together with marinading the chicken 4-5 hours.
(Depends how long you marinade your chick'n.

Get This:

3 pounds of chicken breast, wings or drumsticks - If you use the chicken breast cut them into smaller pieces. Or do not pick just one. Mix it all! Be fierce!

2 1/2 tablespoons freshly ground black pepper - #DadJokeOfTheDay - Why do all witches wear black? So, you cannot tell which witch is which. - Okay I am cancelling myself!

2 1/2 TBS of paprika - For those specimens that do not understand the short-cut of TBS it stands for (Total Bull Sh*t) no I am kidding its Tablespoon......

2 1/2 teaspoons dried oregano - Dried, remarkably like your love life. It is okay... I am here for you.

1 1/2 cups all-purpose flour - All purpose... Should I continue with this joke?

1 teaspoon cayenne pepper - okay let us see if your humor is as dry as mine... Why did Pepper go to prison? A-**SALT** - and just like this we went to another ingredient! What a transition. Also make sure salt is kosher.

1 large egg - There goes Mike running out of the kitchen after you glanced at him reading this ingredient out loud, scared breaking his ankles as he only has ONE EGG LEFT! Poor mike.

3 teaspoons garlic powder - This is totally unrelated. But this just pop out in my head, and I am like why not... So, I hate when you tell people good things like ... I got a new car! And they go oh my gosh my friend crashed hers... Why so negative? I do not go up to a pregnant woman and tell her my dad left. Yaa know. Moving on.

1 cup buttermilk - Okay, so I will ask you this... Where do Russians get milk? ... Think hard! ... MOS-COWS! ... Please do not throw your shoe at me.

1/2 cup cornstarch - Another unrelated bit... As I just saw a big as* spider. You know so many homophobic people turn out to be secretly gay...... so, it makes me nervous I am secretly a giant spider. Since I am so spider phobic. Before you hate my joke, I cannot think straight! Wink!

4 cups vegetable shortening or peanut oil - #DadJokeOfTheDay - What do peanut butter and prostitutes have in common? They both spread for bread...

1 teaspoon baking powder – Just that!

Do This:

GET a bowl out! *(WRONG BOWL TANIA!) LOL!* Combine the paprika, garlic powder, black pepper, oregano, and cayenne in a bowl and mix thoroughly preferably with fork. Mix mix mix!

NOW my beautiful chef! Whisk the egg, buttermilk, 1 tablespoon salt, and 2 tablespoons of the spice mixture in a large bowl. Add the chicken pieces and toss and turn to coat these fuc*ers. Transfer the contents of the bowl to a gallon-sized zipper-lock freezer bag, refrigerate for at least 3-4 hours. If you do not have a zipper-lock bag, use a regular plastic bag.

AFTER 3-4 hours or marinading, whisk together flour, cornstarch, baking powder, 2 teaspoons salt, and the remaining spice mixture in a large bowl that you have got over there. Add 3 tablespoons of the marinade from the zipper-lock bag, work it into the flour with your fingertips, oh gosh here comes your dirty mind. Remove one piece of chicken from the bag, let excess buttermilk to drip off - I am just making this worse visually, am I? drop the chicken into the flour mixture, and toss to coat. Continue adding chicken to the flour mixture one at a time until they are all in the bowl. Toss and turn the chick'n until every piece is thoroughly coated then press it into the flour to make the layer thicker.

SO now adjust an oven rack to the middle position *(I know your favorite)* and preheat the oven to 350-355°F. Heat the shortening/oil to 425°F in a 12-inch straight-sided cast-iron large wok, or a deep pan whatever you got over medium-high heat. Adjust the heat as necessary to maintain the temperature, be damn careful not to let the fat get any hotter like me ;)

SINGLE piece *(that is what they call you)* at a time, transfer the coated chick'n to a fine-mesh strainer and shake to remove excess flour. Shake shake shake! Also, you deserve a glass of wine! Transfer to a wire rack if you do not have one use a plate or whatever you got. Once all the chicken pieces are coated, place in the pan. The temperature should drop to 300°F; adjust the heat to maintain the temperature at 300°F for the duration of the cooking - I know so complicated. Fry the chick'n until it is a deep golden brown on the first side, about 7 minutes; do not move the chicken or start checking for doneness until it has fried for at least 3-4minutes, or you will knock off the coating. So *CAREFUL!* Carefully flip the chicken pieces with thongs I mean tongs... and cook until the second side is golden brown, about 4 minutes longer-ish.

NOW for the finale! Transfer chicken to a baking sheet, season lightly with salt, and place in the oven. Bake until thickest part of breast pieces is at about 150°F on an instant-read thermometer, and if using thigh/drumstick pieces register 165°F, 5 to 10 minutes; remove chicken pieces as they reach their target temperature, and transfer to a second baking sheet, or a paper towel-lined plate. Season with salt to taste. Serve immediately as its banging!

GOSH this was so damn long. Pass me a glass of Wine!

*<u>Disclaimer:</u> This is probably the longest recipe in this book. But it's great! *

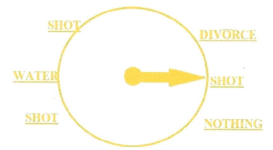

SPIN GAME

I wanted to play a game. It is a spin game. I already went for you! Go on, take that shot.

Pg.43

Stone Fire (hot hot) Chicken veggie naan!
It is easy, international and delicious!

About the dish:

This recipe is quite international because of the naan which originated in greater Iran and central Asia. At least once again that is what uncle internet tells us! Well, this recipe is a random find. This is another *"let us put everything together and see what happens"* - type deal... It came out quite fine to be honest. *Stone fire?* Well, that is what is says on the naan bread package... So, trust the marketing. Or not you choose. I do not care. This blend of flavors and veggies will rock your world! It is quite unusual as its not a pizza nor is it a traditional naan. It is original let us just leave it at that. Pair with your choice of alcohol beverage or water. *Whatever. K bye get going.*

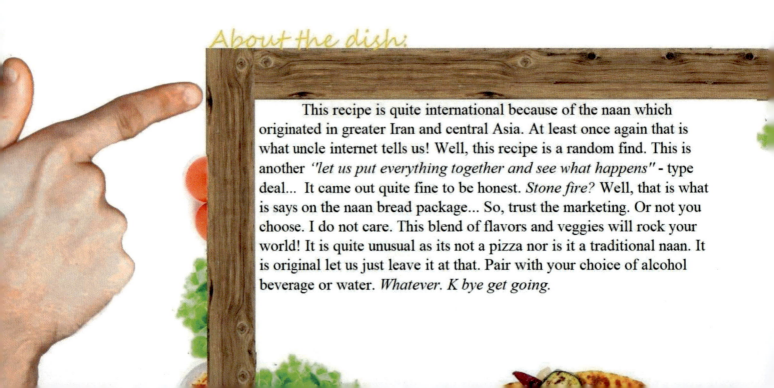

Serving size: 4 Big naans.

Prep time: 5 Minutes

Cook Time: 15 minutes. Give or take!

Get This:

2 packages of large naan bread (most supermarkets have it usually 3-4 per pack they are flat). Just ask someone or go on internet to find it.

2 Chicken large breasts. - Not the super flat ones. This is not that kind of runway! Thick, Thick and once again Thick!

1 shot of vodka... No, not for the recipe for you. You had a long day ... Chug one Becky.

3 Cups of Mozzarella cheese - #DadJokeOfTheDay: What do you get by mixing Mozart and Cinderella? ... Mozzarella...

1 Large onion – Funny story. My friend's son Chris goes... David my mama so scary, the government moved Halloween to her birthday. She stood behind him.

1 Large tomato – Another funny story with Chris... My friend told Chris that he is too young for an iPhone. He goes! You are so old, that when you walked out of a museum on our field trip - the alarm went off. Now he is grounded.

1 Yellow squash – Insert your own joke. I'm tired.

1 tablespoon of butter – Salted, unsalted however you want it. Do not give me that look!

3 tablespoons of garlic - Our favorite breath killer. No kiss for you after this one!

1/2 of a cup Roasted Garlic seasoning. - For the not so mathematically advanced, that's around 2 tablespoons and a half give or take.

Pepper and salt to taste – Sprinkle here and there type of deal.

Fresh parsley as a garnish.

Pg. 45

Do This:

<u>WELL</u>, hello there again beautiful. Let us take those chicken breasts and chop - chop them. Into small pieces. Put it in a bowl and add pepper, salt, and roasted garlic seasoning *(I use McCormick)* mix it all together! Whip out that lovely pan of yours *(it works as a weapon too just FYI in case your spouse pisses you off... But hey you did not hear that from ME!)* and add 2 tablespoons of oil. Heat up, make it sizzle and throw your victim *(the breast)* on it. Fry until cooked through. 5-10 minutes depends on the sizes you had chopped. SET ASIDE.

<u>ONCE</u> the chicken is done, add butter and 2 spoons of garlic into a cup and microwave it until butter melts. If you do not own a microwave, IDK breath on it until it melts. Now, take out your naan bread, take a cooking brush or whatever you call it and dip in the garlic butter mixture and add to the top of each naan. Be generous and if you ran out of it - just make another batch of garlic butter. Now add chicken on top of the naan *(I usually take a fork and shred the chicken with it while on the pan)*, cut yellow squash into slices *(rather thin)* and lay on top of chicken, sprinkle little cheese on top so it does not fall apart, now cut tomatoes and onion same thinner slices and add on top.

<u>SPRINKLE</u> some cheese on each layer. Pretend the chicken and veggies are strippers and mozzarella are $1 singles... if that helps, make it rain HONEEEYYY. I sometimes add mushrooms too, sliced of course tastes GREAT. After you are done add more cheese on top. Heat up your oven to 385F and put your naans on a baking pan and put inside the oven for 6 minutes. Take it out springle with chopped parsley. Voila! Tastes good with ranch, garlic sauce, ketchup, WINE, ETC!

*<u>Disclaimer:</u> I am running low on jokes today. Why? Because I am tired why are you judging. Instead shut up and PASS ME A SHOT instead. *

QUICK GAME

<u>Finish the drawing:</u>

Take your anger out and draw your boss, or someone you do not like. Draw them however you want. After take a shot and laugh about it. *DO NOT DRUNK TEXT THIS TO THEM THOUGH!* And blame me after!
ENJOY!

Beijing Beef
Spicy, delicious, sensational!

About the dish:

Beijing China – this dish is indeed inspired by that part of the world. It is delicious! Seriously! I am not just saying it because this recipe is in my book HA-HA. It truly is slamming! Paired with your choice of rice and it's a perfect dinner choice. Tastes great as a left-over too. This recipe is not difficult! Therefore, I have faith in your abilities. Might want to up that home insurance in case you burn the crap out of your kitchen. K bye.

Pg. 47

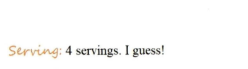

Serving: 4 servings. I guess!

Prep Time: 20 minutes. If you are clumsy - might take longer.

Cook Time: 20 minutes. That is it!

Get This:

1 pound flank steak – Funny story my friend's kid Chris is such a beast! His mommy goes... *Chris you need to eat little less chocolate as you will gain a lot of weight honey!* His reply was: *That is why when you stepped on a scale it said: "To be continued."?*

1 cup canola oil – My friend's kid goes: *My grandpa said grandma is so old, that she was a waitress during the last supper.*

4 cloves garlic minced – Wife to husband: *Ever since I saw you in your family tree I've wanted to cut it down.*

1 yellow onion sliced – My neighbor goes... My sister thought she was so smart; she said the only vegetable/fruit that can make her cry is an onion. So, I threw a coconut at her. DAMN.

1 pieces red bell pepper cut into 1" – If you do not know what 1'' looks like ask your husband. He knows.

1/4 cup cornstarch divided – Divided... Reminds me your divorce. *Too soon?* It's okay plenty of fish in the sea.

1/4 teaspoon salt – Salty as fu*k. Like your EX. True tho! You know it - I know it.

3 egg whites beaten – Wives are like grenades... Remove the ring and boom, a house is gone!

1 teaspoon cornstarch – #DadJokeOfTheDay - Who is the leader of the corn army? The kernel.

1/2 cup water – After last night you might need to chug a bucket! Or two.

1/4 cup sugar – You look like a person that would exchange one of your chromosomes for a Big Mac.

3 tablespoons ketchup – Another funny story. My neighbor Chad goes – *I think my wife is defective... She cried onto a ketchup packet because it said, "tear here."*

6 TBS Hoisin sauce – For the non-bright specimens - *TBS= tablespoon*

1 tablespoon low sodium soy sauce – My dad goes...*What are you drinking, son?* Me: *Soy Milk* Dad: *Hola Milk, soy padre...* Please do not quit your job DAD.

2 teaspoons oyster sauce –Why oysters do not give to charity? Because they are shellfish.

4 teaspoons sweet chili sauce – My grandpa to the neighbor he does not like: *Your forehead is so big you donated it to charity for shelter!*

1 teaspoon crushed red peppers - #AnotherDadJokeOfTheDay - *What do you call two spices saying hello to each other during the holidays? Season's greetings.* I know these slowly get worse.

Do This:

HELLO there my lovely chefs! Please cut the damn flank steak against the grain into thin 1/4-inch slices. Then, in a medium bowl add - beef, egg, salt and 1 teaspoon cornstarch. Let marinate for 30 minutes up to an hour. The more the better!

How to make Beijing Beef Sauce: In a small bowl whisk together the 1/2 cup water, 1/4 cup sugar, ketchup, hoisin, soy sauce, oyster sauce, sweet chili sauce, crushed red peppers and apple cider vinegar. MIX!

AFTER our lovely beef has finishing marinating add 2 tablespoons cornstarch to a bowl, add marinated beef *(discard the extra marinade)*. Moving on!

GET a medium sauce pan out and heat it up with the oil on medium/high. Use more oil if needed. With the last two tablespoons of cornstarch toss the beef one last time and shake off any excess cornstarch.

NOW for the halftime show… Fry the slices, in batches, until golden brown *(3-4 minutes)*. Heat a large pan on high heat, use 2 tablespoons of oil you just fried the beef in. Now add onion and bell pepper - cook for 3-4 minutes, until it just starts caramelizing on the edges. Afterwards, add the garlic in and continue to cook a few more seconds until fragrant.

REMOVE all veggies and put them with beef on a plate. Add Beijing Beef sauce to a large pan and cook on high until it thickens, about 3-5 minutes. Might take few minutes more!

FINALLY! Add beef and vegetables into the sauce, toss to combine. Serve with fried rice! Quick recipe below.

Quick Fried Rice Recipe: Prepare 2 cups of white rice. Heat 1/2 tablespoon (7ml) vegetable oil in a pan over high heat until smoking. Add half of rice and cook, stirring and tossing, until the rice is pale brown and toasted and has a lightly chewy texture, about 3 minutes! Transfer to a medium bowl. Repeat with another 1/2 tablespoon oil and remaining rice. After you finish, transfer all rice into the pan. Add 1 onion, 2 carrot, 2 scallions (chopped), and garlic and cook, stirring gently, until lightly softened and fragrant, about 1 minute. Toss with rice to combine. Add soy sauce and sesame oil and toss to coat. Season to taste with salt and white pepper. Push rice to the side of the wok and add 1/2 tablespoon (7ml) oil. Break 1 egg into the oil and season with a little salt. Use a spatula to scramble the egg, breaking it up into small bits. Toss the egg and the rice together. Add frozen peas and continue to toss and stir until peas are thawed and every grain of rice is separate. Serve immediately.

GAME: If you have a dice at home. Roll it. Whatever you roll - you have to do what says below. IF you do not have a dice. Go to a app store on your phone. Im sure there is a dice app.

- ⚀ **Person to your right drinks** — If you are alone. Sorry you gotta take this.
- ⚁ **Person to your left drinks** — Just like the one above.
- ⚂ **You take a shot**
- ⚃ **Pour someone a shot** — If you are alone. You fu*ked yourself over.
- ⚄ **You take two shots**
- ⚅ **Everyone takes a shot** — Again if its just you. Take one.

*<u>Disclaimer:</u> You are welcome for the rice. Also, do not burn your kitchen! *

Pg. 49

Qucik Chick'n Parmesan
Delicious & Qucik

About the dish:

Ahhh! Chicken parmesan! What is more Italian that this. My hand automatically goes:

I should just leave this at that!

This is my special quick recipe. It is quite simple and does not require massive amounts of ingredients. Chicken parm is an extremely popular Italian dish. You know it, I know it, your mom *know's it!* Therefore, get your cute butt ready!

Get This:

Servings: 6 humans, 1 dog, no cats AMY!
Prep Time: 20 minutes give or take!
Cook Time: 30 minutes.

4 boneless, skinless chicken breasts - #DadJokeOfTheDay - What does a baby computer call his father? Data.

4 cups of mozzarella cheese - Which is the saddest cheese? Prov-Alone. He's always alone.

2 Cups of Parmesan cheese — #AnotherDadJokeOfTheDay - Why didn't the cheese want to get sliced? -- It had grater plans... LAME I KNOW!

1 ½ 24oz Marinara sauce – <u>My grandpa goes:</u> *How does pizza sauce introduce itself at a fiesta?* <u>ME:</u> *I don't know! What?* <u>Grandpa:</u> *Yo soy marinara.*

4 cloves of minced garlic — Rest in peace - You will be minced!

½ cup of basil & ½ cup oof parsley – Only cups can help you. You suck at math. Get them cups SON!

2 cups of breadcrumbs - I usually use flavored ones mixed with panko.

2 cups of flour – Cat lady goes: *What kind of flour should you use to make a cake for a cat?* <u>All purr-puss flour</u>. Oh my….

2 Eggs – What is the difference between you and egg? Egg gets laid, you do not.

Metal medium baking pan...Also 1 TBS of salt and pepper.

Do This: *<u>Disclaimer:</u> Please do not burn yourself! Clumsy! *

CUT breasts in half horizontally. Pound them thin. Once done, crack eggs into a big bowl add parsley, 4 cloves of minced garlic, 1TBS of pepper and salt. Let it sit for 15 minutes.

AFTER this process is done. Get another medium bowl. Mix breadcrumbs and flour together. Heat up a medium size pan add some oil. Now take each breast, and coat it with breadcrumbs and flour mixture. Then fry on medium, 4-5 minutes each side until golden brown or until the chicken is done.

GET baking pan out, pour some marinara sauce on bottom. After, lay down fried chicken breasts. spread 2 cups of mozzarella cheese and 1 cup of parmesan cheese. Sprinkle half of your basil on top. Now, pour remaining marinara sauce on top. Add remaining cheese and basil on top. Bake on 350F for only 8-10 minutes. **SERVE** over pasta.

Welcome to Mom

Who Is SHE!

Dorota Milewski – My wonderful mother like no other! This woman raised me to be who I am today. I think she did a great job despite being a single mother. Hard working, very loving, smart, funny and beautiful. I could have tons of words to describe her. She installed courage and ability to dream in me. I know it is cliché to say that a parent is loving. However, my mother's love extends not only to me but to many people she meets. She is the first one to get you dancing and laughing! Her hospitality extends the norms! Therefore, in this chapter I will present to you her top 3 traditional main dishes picks! She and I hope you will like them. Enjoy!

Enjoy!

Polish Golombki
(pron. GO-WOM-PKI) don't mess up with the pronunciation!
(Stuffed Cabbage Rolls) Tasty & Healthy

About the dish:

Hello lovely chefs! Here we have a truly authentic traditional Polish dish! It is my mom's and grandmas special! It is little time consuming but super worth it. It is healthy - for the healthy freaks reading this. Yes, Linda you will not gain much weight eating this. Originated in Kingdom of Poland (current Poland) in the 18th century. Some of you might remember the date... JOKE! Just kidding! I grew up eating this dish. Each time it is made, and my non-polish friends try it they love it! Give it a go! This dish is made in bigger batches. YES, you can freeze it! Usually tastes better next day anyways! Great for a hungover! Ask my aunt Linda. She's been practicing this hungover method since 1970's

Pg. 53

Get This:

Serving Size: About 15 cabbage rolls.

Prep Time: 35 Minutes. My mom is watching. Do not screw this up.

Cook time: 1 hour and 30 minutes! Kind of long, kind of worth it.

1 Medium metal cooking tray - Get them at any $ store in the area! Unless you have casserole dish with cover... use that then!

1 medium white cabbage - Try to find one with large leaves, as these are the ones we will use!

500 g ground turkey dark meat, approx. 7% fat - #DadJokeOfTheDay - What do you call a turkey on the day after Thanksgiving? Lucky! - Don't sue me. It is just sh*t and giggles!

140 g rice (¾ cup) - I am halfway through becoming a stand-up comedian. I can already stand up, now all I need is comedy...... Unfair I know.

300 ml water for boiling the rice - #AnotherDadJokeOfTheDay - In what direction does a chicken swim? Cluck-wise! - okay ... I am done.

1 onion finely chopped – Funny but real story… I loved onions as a kid… That it became my nickname. My bowl haircut did not help neither.

2 tbsp olive oil - If you do not have olive oil... You know the drill... Any would do!

1 tsp fine sea salt plus plenty of pepper - This is unrelated to the ingredient but... My mom goes... *do you know your grandpa tried to warn everyone that the Titanic will sink.* I responded... *WOW I did not know grandpa was around then...* Then she goes... *When everyone just ignored him, he yelled at them three more times. Eventually, they got irritated and we got kicked the fu*k out of the theater...* I do not know what is worse... This joke? Or the fact I thought my grandpa was over 100!

FOR THE SAUCE

3 tbsp tomato passata - For the non-bright specimens TBSP stands for tablespoon.

2 tbsp tomato puree – No joke here. Just nag for a shot!

300 ml chicken/vegetable stock hot - Hot, yes that used to be your relationship. Now it's just dry like the next ingredient.

1/2 tbsp of basil - Read above... I was not kidding.

Do This:

I WILL keep this joke free. As it is long, and I do not want you to mess this fuc*er up. So, fasten your seatbelts! By seatbelts I meant take a deep shot of your choice of booze... Let's go!

PLACE cabbage in a large pot filled with water so the cabbage can get covered with it (cut end of the cabbage down), cover and bring to boil. After, lower the heat and simmer gently for about 10 minutes, covered, until the outer leaves start separating.

MEANWHILE cabbage is simmering rinse the rice thoroughly. Then, combine with 1 and ¼ cup of lightly salted water, cover and bring to the boil. Lower the heat and simmer for about 10 minutes, covered, until all the water has been absorbed. Place in a large bowl and set aside to cool.

REMOVE cabbage from the pot (Be careful its hot, use a fork and try to separate leaves.) Carefully place the loose leaves on a plate. Put the cabbage back in the pot, continue simmering, then remove a few more leaves. Repeat until you have got about 18-20 leaves.

TAKE out a frying pan heat up the oil, add the onion and cook over a low heat for about 4-5 minutes until softened and golden. Mix with the rice, then set aside in a bowl.

PREHEAT the oven to 350F. Line a large casserole dish (or metal cooking pan) with cabbage leaves (the small ones or ones that have torn) and set aside.

USING a sharp knife slice off the thick bit running along the length of the cabbage leaf on the outside like this!

Be careful not to split the leaf.
Do this for each leaf.

MIX - rice, onion mixture (once cooled) and meat, about 1 teaspoon of fine sea salt, add plenty of pepper. Create a good size oval shaped meatball and place in the leaf.

TO BE CONTINUED ON THE NEXT PAGE!.....

Continuation.

HOW TO MAKE A CABBAGE ROLL: fold in the longer sides, then wrap the filling starting with the thick end of the leaf. Press the mixture in with your fingers as you are rolling and roll as tightly as possible. Place the cabbage rolls one by one in deep metal baking pan or casserole dish so they are tight together. If you cannot figure how to roll it. Ask your neighbor or wife. Or look at this!

TO MAKE THE SAUCE: Combine hot stock with the passata and tomato paste & stir thoroughly. Pour this mixture over the cabbage rolls. Cover with a sheet of non-stick paper cut to fit the shape of your dish (or small leaves if there are any left), then cover with a lid or tin foil and bake in the center of the oven for 1hour and 30 minutes. *TIP:* Golombki taste the best while they cool off and get reheated after few hours as the sauce gets more time to bind into the roll.

***Disclaimer:** No pigeons were harmed in this recipe. Why pigeons? Golombki translate to Pigeon... See now you learned some Polish... However, don't use this in your resume. *

My mom said you desevre a shot!

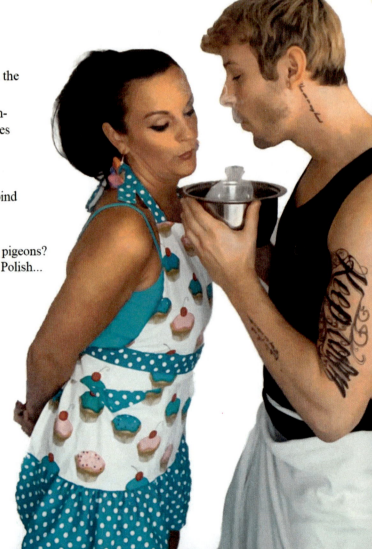

Authentic Fried Polish Pierogi
Not that BS kind. It is not Pierogies!
(How to correctly pronounce it - pih-eh-ro-ge.)

About the dish:

    This is probably one of the most famous Polish recipes out there. Both my mother and grandmother made their own. It makes me proud that we have created a dish so popular that is eaten throughout the world. So, if you have not tried a truly authentic version yet, then definitely give these a-go. These are the real deal straight off a pole. *(Not a stripper's pole... Pole is what a Polish person is named in English language you non cultured specimen).* It always makes me laugh when people mispronounce this dish. Pirogi, Perogis, Peregis... I think I have heard all different types by now, CUT THAT SHI*. *International lesson #1* - Put that wine glass down and pay damn attention. It is pronounced *"pih-eh-ro-ge"*. Okay? Got it? Perfect! Let us move on. To make this dish, you need patience ... If you do not have patience, take 2 shots and your perception shall change. Unless you are an angry drinker than a half-folded pierogi might fly thru the kitchen. Let's go! Remember my mom's watching!

Servings: 8 unless you are me - A great white whale who devours food like its air - so that is 3 servings.

Prep Time: 2 hours - do not get discouraged. Good things take time.

Cook Time: 30 minutes - not so bad, is it?

Resting Time: 30 minutes - yes you need to let them rest after boiling, so they are ready for some sizzle drizzle on the pan.

Get This:

FOR THE FILLING:

5 Potatoes yellow, medium or 3 large russet potatoes - Peel them nicely. #DadJokeOfTheDay - What do you call a lazy spud? A couch potato. Or in other words your husband. YES, I SAID IT RONALD GET YOUR A*S UP! (You can insert name of your choosing unless your husband's name is Ronald...).

8 oz Farmer cheese - This you can find in any supermarket. Just ask someone. You never heard of it? What a coincidence your celebrity crush never heard of you, yet you exist. It is what it is Becky.

1 sweet, yellow, large, chopped onion - I will leave this alone. Joke free. You are already filing that joke spot anyways.

1/2 teaspoon Garlic - *How old is Mary?* My friend's dad: David, my wife is so old that when she farts, dust comes out. - *Not the answer I was looking for.*

1/2 teaspoon Onion powder - Mary being Mary did not wait and clapped back: Well Richard is old that he co-wrote the Ten Commandments. - *Don't F* with Mary*

1 tablespoon Oil for onion - Any damn oil. Be reckless... Like college kids on budget.

Kosher salt and freshly ground black pepper to taste.

FOR THE DOUGH:

3 cups Whole purpose flour - Once again Sniffany, please sit down it's just flour.

1/2 cup Milk 2%, warm - Just pop that fuc*er in a microwave for like 20 seconds.

1/2 to 3/4 cup WARM water (depending on how much your flour soaks) - The goal of the dough is to not be watery! Do not mess up AMY! I know you are reading this.

1 tablespoon Butter melted, unsalted - Husband: *I'm trying to imagine you with a personality.* Wife's reply: *You're IQ's lower than your shoe size.*

Do This:

FOR THE FILLING:

Place potatoes in a pot, cover with water and cook until fork tender. In the meantime, heat up the oil in a frying pan, add onions and cook until golden brown. Once potatoes are cooked, using a potato ricer or potato masher *(If you do not have any of these, why the hell are you cooking...)*, mash the potatoes so they do not have any lumps. Add farmer cheese and mix, onions, all spices from filling section, salt, and pepper and mix well. MIX MIX MIX! Take a damn shot break! AYYYE! You deserve it. You made it this far!

FOR THE DOUGH:

Pour flour into a large bowl, add a pinch of salt. Make a little hole in a middle and start adding milk and butter. Add a little warm water work the dough until it becomes soft and elastic until you can form a ball about 10-15 minutes. *MAKE SURE ITS NOT WATERY* – add more flour if needed. Get to work. This is probably your only workout in a day anyways. Polish cuisine is hard labor! But worth it!

ONCE done, cover it and let it rest for about 20-30 minutes. Roll the dough until thin *(like pasta)* and using either cookie cutter or large wine glass cut the circles. I hope you know your shapes... *Stares at you Sean*... This is not a fuc*ing circle. THIS IS !

PLACE 1 teaspoon of the filling in the middle of the circle, picture above! Wet one half of the circle and then seal it together. Use a fork or fingers and press the end to seal the pierogi like photo above. It gives that nice design - WHO ARE YOU Picasso!?!? After this you might be.

BOIL large pot of water and season with salt. Once the water is boiling put about 8 pierogi at the time. Once they come to the surface let them cook for 1 minute and using a spider or slotted spoon take them out on a plate. Once again if you do not have any of these, figure it out.

IMPORTANT: After pierogis are boiled let them air dry. Once this step is done. Take out a frying pan. Add some oil, and fry pierogies on medium/high until golden brown.

CONTINUE TO THE NEXT PAGE!

Continuation:

FRY about 2-3 Minutes on each side. Serve with salt and pepper to taste! They are yummy!

TIP: Pierogi can also be eaten boiled with bacon and onion fried on butter. To do so. Get some fresh bacon out fry it and crumble it, add 1 onion finely chopped. After, pour it over boiled pierogies. Top with sour cream and chopped scallions.

Disclaimer: WOW, you managed it through. Sh*t so proud of you. You learned how to make a banging dish and got little cultured along the way. Congratulations, hopefully you did this correctly if not, buy extra sh*t paper... Might need it. My mom is proud of your accomplishment. *

My mom is proud of you!
Take a shot for her!

   Or two!

Polish Placki Ziemniaczane (Potato pancakes)

Try them – they are fuc*ing awesome. Your mom said so too!

About the dish:

Potato! If you can sum me up into one word it would be a POTATO! Why? Because I eat it so much. I grew up on this recipe as it is so delicious! Potatoes for Polish cuisine are like rice to Spanish cuisine. We use it for everything! This is an authentic Polish recipe for potato pancakes! With side sauce! Placki ziemniaczane - a food staple at the 17th-century for Polish monasteries, and well peasants in the Kingdom of Poland *(Today Poland)!* Mainly because it did not require many ingredients and was easy & cheap to make. This is truly a simple but delicious dish! Give it a try! Make my mom proud! Just because it was a food for mostly peasants at the time does not mean you are not one today. Joke… I mean Is it? If we went back in time, I am sure most of us middle class people will qualify as peasants.

Also, look at it this way. If there was ever the end of the world crisis this recipe can come in handy! Go give it a try! Why not. Open yourself to international cuisine!

Servings: 6 peasants, 3 dogs, 1 horse and absolutely no cats.

Prep Time: 30-45 mins- give or take!

Cook Time: 15 mins – easy breezy!

Get This:

6 medium potatoes peeled and finely grated. - #DadJokeOfTheDay - *Who is the most powerful potato?* Darth Tater. Eh starting lame… *BOO DAVID YOU SUCK!*

1 medium onion finely grated. – Fun fact! Anyone who thinks onions are the only vegetable that makes you cry… Has clearly never been hit in the face with a turnip. Do not try this at home!

2 large eggs – My grandpa goes… What does an EGG and YOU have in common? Me: *I don't know, what!*…….Grandpa: *Actually nothing because egg gets laid – you don't.*

Kosher salt, to taste – My friend's wife goes: Q. *Why are men like diapers?* A. *They're usually full of sh*t, but thankfully disposable.* Ouch Becky!

Scallions - The same wife from above goes to her husband: You have two parts of brain, *'left'* and *'right'*. In the left side, there's nothing right. In the right side, there's nothing left. He replied: *I'd like to see things from your point of view but I can't seem to get my head that far up my ass.* They are still married.

Freshly ground pepper, to taste - My neighbor's kid goes: *My momma such a bad cook, she uses the smoke alarm as a timer.* Damn.

2/3 cup vegetable oil, for frying – Do not spill oil while frying. You cannot even afford insurance. I know it - you know it.

1/4 cup all-purpose flour, more as needed. - #AnotherDadJokeOfTheDay - Jonny played in the mud. *Then* Jonny took a bath with bubbles. *You want to hear a dirty joke?* Bubbles was the next-door neighbor.

Garnish: sour cream + Maggi seasoning – Seasoning can be found in any big grocery stores. It is not a powder form. It is in a bottle, resembles soy sauce in color. ASK SOMEONE!

Seasoning looks like this:
For the copyright reasons the name is not visible.

Do This:

IN a large mixing bowl, mix potatoes, onion, eggs, salt, and pepper. MIX! MIX! MIX! Add enough flour to bind the mixture together while leaving it somewhat thin. Something like this:

IN a large, heavy skillet set over medium-high heat, add vegetable oil to a depth of 1/4-inch. Heat until hot, but make sure it is not smoking. Afterwards, drop tablespoonfuls of potato mixture into the skillet and spread out to form a 3-inch circle that is about 1/4-inch thick.

HOWEVER, you do not have to be precise! Fry until brown on the bottom *(do not turn until the pancake is brown or it will stick)*, about 2 to 5 minutes. If needed, reduce the heat to medium to prevent burning. Once this is done, turn the pancake and fry the other side for 2 to 5 minutes or until golden brown and crisp. Drain on paper towels.

WAYS TO SERVE -ON THE NEXT PAGE:

Ways To Serve:

PANCAKES can be served with the sauce made of 1 cup of sour cream, and about 3TBS of Maggi seasoning. MIXED, add more sour cream or Magii if needed. (Sauce should be light brown).

ALSO, can be served with mushroom sauce to make sauce you will need: 1 tablespoon vegetable oil (I used olive oil), 1 small onion - finely chopped, 1 teaspoon butter, 1 ½ Cup white mushrooms - sliced, juice of ½ lemon, ½ Cup of vegetable or chicken stock, 1 Cup sour cream, Some dill for garnish, *How To Make It:* Heat the oil in a frying pan over a low heat and fry the onions for 4 minutes, until golden and soft. Add the butter along with the mushrooms and cook for a further 2 minutes, until soft. Add the lemon juice. Pour in the stock and simmer for 1 minute, then stir in the sour cream and leave to bubble and simmer for 2-3 minutes, until slightly thickened.

CAN be served with any type of gravy as well.

CAN be served with sour cream and scallions

WITH warm applesauce.

OR wrap it with one of the books salads: Either cabbage salad or taco salad. Works well with fried chicken and sauce of choice.

SO MANY CHOICES EHH?

TRY THEM ALL!

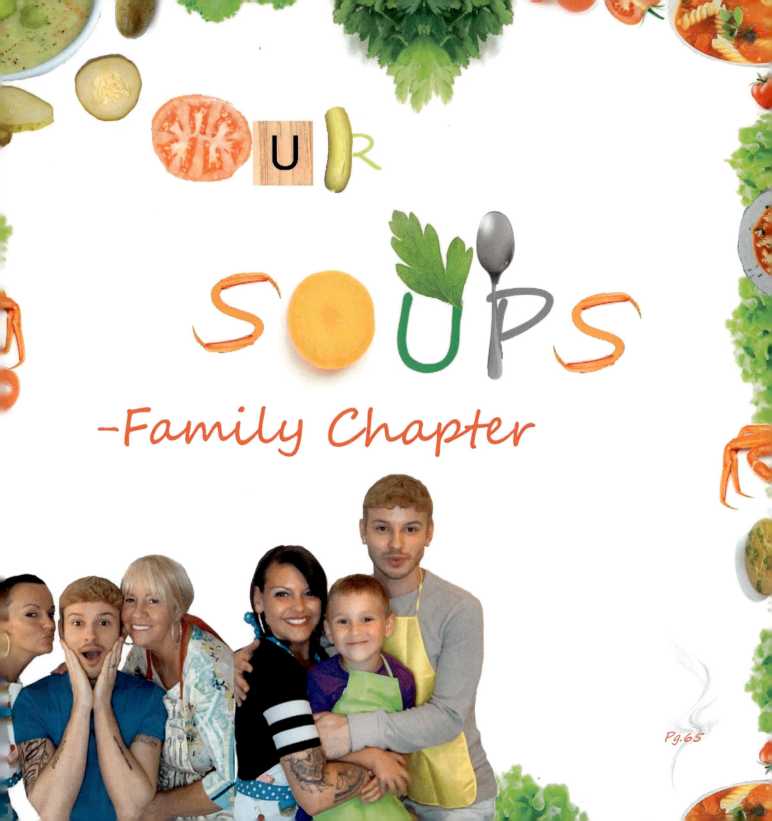

Our Soups
–Family Chapter

Pg. 65

NOT SO SHY TOMATO SOUP!

*Family style. Notice: * This is not a thick soup. But damn good!*

About the dish:

This is both my grandmas and mom's special old recipe done by me! It is a healthy soup. Good for breakups, sad days & hang overs and whatever you need it for. *I grew up on it*. Therefore, make sure you follow all the steps – so it does not come out as a FLOP! This is not your typical thick soup as Polish soups tend to be waterier rather than dense. This soup is totally great! Paired either with noodles or cooked rise is to die for. This soup came to Poland from Italy some hundreds of years ago. Polish people changed the recipe and made the recipe its own. Try it out! *Smacznego! – That is how you say ''Bon appetite'' in Polish.* See you are becoming so… International.

Serving: 5-6 People perhaps.

Prep Time: 10-15 minutes. Not so long.

Cook Time: 40-60 Minutes

Pasta any choice - Angel hair - I do not care, shells, penne, any will do. ALSO pairs great with cooked white rice! YUMMY.

Get This:

2 Chicken Dumbbells or 2 Chicken wings RAW - Insert your own joke Billy. You know you want to.

2 TBS of tomato paste - Pretend it's a shark attack when you drop it into the water...

half a teaspoon of sugar, 1 Teaspoon of all spice, 1 teaspoon of salt. – Yes Im running out of space.

2 Large carrots - My friend's wife got upset at him the other day and said: *If laughter is the best medicine, your face must be curing the world.* He of course clapped back: *What language are you speaking? Cause it sounds like bullsh*t.* She ended this conversation with: *I'm jealous of all the people that haven't met you!* He replied: *Stupidity is not a crime so you are free to go.* They are happily married!

1/4 cup of chopped parsley – This lady at the store argued with some man. I assumed it was her relative... She yelled: *You are proof that evolution CAN go in reverse assho*e.* He yelled back: *Moses called for the dollar you owe him lady.*

1/2 cups of sour cream! – #DadJokeOfTheDay - Q: *What is a dead man's favorite magazine?* A: *Life.*

1/2 cups of celery - I asked my friend's kid how old is grandpa. He replied: *So old that he still has his fork from the first super.*

1 Bay Leaf -Me: *Dad explain to me solar eclipse.* Dad: *No Sun* - Get it?

1 teaspoon of black pepper - If you do not have spoons, Idk measure by eye. Unless your eyesight is F*cked up. Then I don't know what to tell you.

1 medium onion! - Survived 2020? you can survive cutting an onion.

2 cloves of garlic... Promoting social distancing ... your loved one will stay 6 feet away!

Half of one leek around 1 cup do not chop. <- MAKE SURE YOU DONT LEEK ...

9 Cups of water - Funny observation! vodka+water = not good for kidneys, rum+water= not good for liver, whiskey+water= not good for heart.... As you see drink water at your own risk!

2 TBS of tomato paste - Pretend it's a shark attack when you drop it into the water...

1 TBS of all-purpose flour - If you like them thick, put more... BUT WAIT try it the way it was mean to be eaten... Little watery!

Pg.67

Before we move on:
NOW TAKE A SHOT LIKE A TRUE POLISH PERSON! YOU DESERVE IT!

NA ZDROWIE! – Cheers in Polish!

DO THIS:

WASH the chicken, whichever decapitated part you used. Whip out that nice size pot. Drop your victims body parts in it, put all the water in it, add all spice, pepper, bay leaf. Boil for 30 minutes on low/medium.

GET all the veggies ready. Peel the ones needing peeling. Cut into big pieces. Add to the pot after you boiled the chicken for 30 minutes. Boil until the veggies are semi soft. Then, add tomato paste, salt, and sugar.

IN a small bowl, mix sour cream with flour. Make sure you stir it until flour and sour cream combines. To the bowl add 2 TBS of the boiled soup you are making & stir. Add back into the soup, stir for 3 minutes.

TAKE the soup off the burner, Cr*p be careful! Take a spoon and try the flavor. If needed add more pepper or salt. The soup tastes better if it stands and cools down for an hour after being boiled. Kind of like the joke... The older the berry the better the juice... Okay after reading this back this is not how the joke went. Serve over pasta noodles or rice (whatever you chose and cooked aside) with load of fresh chopped parsley.

READ THE DISCLAIMER IT IS SUPER IMPORTANT

*<u>Disclaimer:</u> I should have told you in the beginning to boil the pasta or rice on the side. Now you came to the end of this recipe, and you are mad as hell, that I did not mention that. Well, I am still editing. I could of just easily fix it. But its funnier this way sorry not sorry! *

Chicken DOODLE DOO Soup
Polish MOM Style!

About the dish:

Personally, I am not a big fan of thick soups. It is like eating baby food all over again, at least to me. No offense to those who enjoy it. This is more liquidly type of soup. With pasta noodles - I like when things float in my soup. Specialty of my mom Dorota *(Eng. Dorothy)* of course as this recipe is hers! Little fact! Rosół is a traditional Polish meat soup. Its most popular variety is the rosół z kury, or clear chicken soup. It is commonly served with capellini pasta. A vegetarian version can be made, substituting meat with oil or butter. It is one of the most popular Polish soups and is served during family dinners as well as a traditional soup for weddings. It is also said to be a great remedy if one catches a cold. *(Rosół – pronunciation is Row-Sawl)*. See, this book not only makes you international it also teaches you history and language! How nice! Well, go ahead and enjoy this soup! If you have a hang-over this works like charm!

Serving Size: Perhaps 8

Prep time: 20 minutes. Clear explanation. To the point. For once!

Cooking time: 45-1hour... Long time? Well Rome was not built in a day... Run 10 laps

Get This:

2 Chicken Dumbbells or 2 Chicken wings RAW - #DadJokeOfTheDay - What do you call a bird who is too afraid to fly? A chicken! I know I am lame! Give me some credit though!

2 Large carrots - Hold the carrot up. Stare at your bf or husband and READ THIS OUT LOUD --->At least something is large in this house! Please record his reaction for me.

1/4 cup of chopped parsley – My friend to her husband: *I can always tell when you are lying. Your lips move.*

1 teaspoon of black pepper - Same friend from above. Her: *Hey, you have something on your chin... no, the 3rd one down.* Her husband replied: *If I had a face like yours, I'd sue my parents.* It is never boring with them!

1 medium onion! – Here is a tissue! Your makeup is about to get fu*ked up.

2 cloves of garlic - #AnotherDadJokeOfTheDay - What does garlic do when it gets hot? It takes its cloves off. LAME! Ha-Ha!

Half of one leek - Leek... Once you pass 30's you leak here and there.

9 Cups of water - You know they say body is made of 90% of water so, I am not fat I am just WATERLOGGED! *You are doing great! *

2 Bay Leaves- BAYYYYYYY you cute. Stare at your boo make up for the carrot joke! When he says thanks… Say I ''Wasn't talking about you''.

1 teaspoon of salt. - My mom once said to my dad: *If bullshit could float...you'd be the Admiral of the fleet!* Anyone can relate?

Pasta any choice... Angel hair - I do not care, shells, penne, any will do. Also, I want to share a new saying I learned! It goes: *Roses are red, Violets are blue. I've got five fingers, The middle one is for you.*

Take a shot and move onto the next page !

If you are underage kindly disregard this message and get yourself a damn juice box.

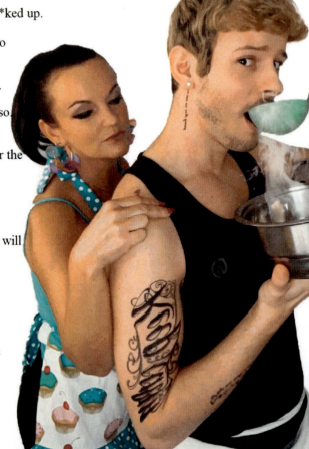

Do This:

WHIP out one of your nice pots... I know you got that one special one. And if you do not umm ehh... Anyways moving on ... Make the water bubble add the raw chicken... add the veggies, all the spices just dump everything into that damn pot. Put the lid on... you do not have one? Hopeless. Well anyways put the lid and leave on low/medium heat and leave it like that for 45 mins. Long time? Well do some push ups to kill some time. Or whatever!

BOIL the pasta: add some salt dump the box of pasta into the hot water, boil it... when ready get it out of the water give it a COLD AS SHOWER set aside. Once your Soup above is done, add pasta to a bowl, then add the soup. ENJOY works great with white rice too! Garnish with fresh parsley or dill! You are welcome!

*__DISCLAIMER:__ This is a healthy soup. Good for when you feel like crap. Or when you are hungover. At least that is what my mom says. They say- always listen to mom, mom knows best! *

__GAME:__ Pick a box.

Flip the book to reveal answers!

If you picked *YELLOW*: Drink if you haven't had S*X in over a week.
If you picked *ORANGE*: You do not have to do anything. It is already hard to own a face like this.
If you picked *GREEN*: You are obligated to take 2 shots of liquor.

Pg. 71

HOLY-MOLY PICKLE SOUP...
Polish Pickled Cucumber Soup. Honestly deserves a culinary award itself.

About the dish:

This is one of my childhood favorites. Done by both my mom and grandma. It is a super delicious authentic old polish style soup. No not nail polish... Polish as in nationality. *(For the not so informed human specimens. Take out a map, or a globe or whatever that shows the world. Go to Europe, see Poland? This soup comes from there).* Credit for this recipe is given to my grandmother Teresa *(Eng. Theresa)*. Fun fact! ZUPA OGÓRKOWA *pron. zoopa ogurkova (Eng. Pickle Soup)* is a traditional and popular Polish soup. "Zupa" means soup in Polish, and "ogorkowa" is the adjectival form of "ogórek," which means "cucumber." The soup is named after the soup's main ingredient: kiszone ogorki, or pickled cucumbers. Traditional Polish meals always begin with a starter, soup being one of the most common. So, zupa ogorkowa would be served before the main course of the meal.

Servings: 6 humans, 2 cats.
Prep Time: 10 MIN or so…
Cook Time: 40 MIN… It is not that long!

Get This:

About 1.5 lbs. / 700g of chicken (wings or other parts) – My grandpa goes: *I'm multi-talented: I can talk and piss you off at the same time.* Grandpa replied: *If sh*t was music, you'd be an orchestra.*

1 tsp salt – I remember when I moved to America and I was in my English class, teacher: *Use the word Dandelion in a sentence* Me without knowing much English then: *Da Cheetah is faster Dandelion.* She was not impressed.

5 bay leaves - #DadJokeOfTheDay - What do you call a seagull that flies over the bay? A bagel… Okay I know super lame… I will show myself out.

6-10 pepper corns whole – I love French accent. When some say Paper, it sounds like PEPPER.

4-6 allspice seeds, whole or a dash of ground allspice – My first-grade teacher told me sarcasm wouldn't get me anywhere. Guess she was right.

3 medium potatoes - #AnotherDadJokeOfTheDay - What do you call a potato at a football game? A spec-tater. David come on… you can do better.

One jar of pickles in brine - My neighbor goes: *I had a crazy dream last night! I was swimming in an ocean of orange soda. Turns out it was just a Fanta sea.* Frank do not quit your job for commedy……

About 3 tbs of fresh dill – My friend's marriage is like a commedy show. He goes: *Whatever kind of look you were going for, you missed.* His wife replied: *The janitor said he took out the trash last night, he must forgot a piece, what are you still doing here?* He replied: *If I had a dollar for every time you said something smart, I'd be broke.* She was not finished, and said: *Your di*k is so small you could use it to floss teeth.* You guessed she won the argument.

3 tbs of flour + 1 c of cold water – If I tell you I'm thinking about you, don't get too excited, because I'm also thinking about nachos.

Pg. 73

Do This:

TAKE A SHOT! BE A TRUE POLISH PERSON. VODKA IS LIKE BLOOD!

THIS will be quick. Wash chicken parts and place in a medium pot with about 6-7 cups (1.5 quarts) of water. Add salt, bay leaves, carrots, pepper corns and allspice. Boil on medium to medium-low heat for about 20 min (until chicken falls off the bone).

MEANTIME, peel potatoes and cube into medium size cubes. If you do not know what cubes look like, then I am sorry for you. Shred pickles on the medium vegetable shredder, set aside. Cut up fresh dill. If you do not have shredder mince it as much as you can.

WHEN chicken is done, remove from stock and take off the bone. Also remove carrots and slice. Add cubed potatoes to the stock and boil for about 10 min, or until soft. When potatoes are soft, return meat and carrots to the pot. Add shredded pickles. Yummy!

IN a small bowl or cup combine cold water with flour, whisk well and add to the soup to thicken a little bit. Bring to boil and turn off. CHOP FRESH DILL!

AND that is it!

*_Disclaimer:_ You might get addicted to this soup if you are pickle lover like me. *

- ⚀ Take a shot of hot sauce
- ⚁ Take a shot of liquor
- ⚂ Take a shot of ketchup.
- ⚃ Venmo me 100$. JK take 2 shots of liquor.
- ⚄ Do 10 push ups.
- ⚅ Say 3 awkwars truths. Or take 3 deep shots. If you are alone. Well... sorry to say 3 shots it is!

GAME: Roll the dice. If you do not have one go to the app store. I am sure there is an app for that. It is 21's century after all! Anyways, whatever number you roll - says what you have to do.

Crazy CRAB! SOUP!
Oh lala

About the dish:

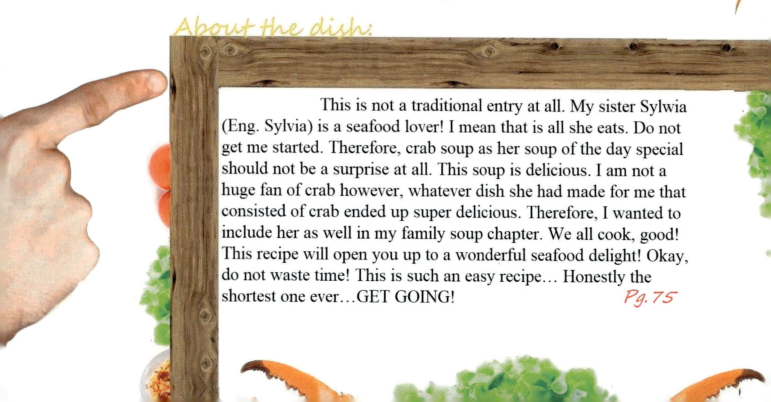

This is not a traditional entry at all. My sister Sylwia (Eng. Sylvia) is a seafood lover! I mean that is all she eats. Do not get me started. Therefore, crab soup as her soup of the day special should not be a surprise at all. This soup is delicious. I am not a huge fan of crab however, whatever dish she had made for me that consisted of crab ended up super delicious. Therefore, I wanted to include her as well in my family soup chapter. We all cook, good! This recipe will open you up to a wonderful seafood delight! Okay, do not waste time! This is such an easy recipe… Honestly the shortest one ever…GET GOING!

Pg. 75

Serving: 4 grown adults, 1 child, 1 donkey I mean your husband.

Prep Time: 5 minutes only!

Cook Time: 15 minutes only! WOW! Stop wasting time get going.

Get this:

1 can (28 ounces) whole tomatoes, cut into small pieces- For this you will need a knife. It is that sharp metal thingy in your kitchen. Please do not chop of your finger. Both you and I know you cannot afford insurance at this moment.

3 cups water- #DadJokeOfTheDay - A friend dug a hole in the garden and filled it with water. I think he meant well. – Okay lame again, sh*t I am trying!

2 cups beef broth- #AnotherDadJokeOfTheDay - What do you call a cow that has two legs shorter on one side of its body compared to the other? LEAN BEEF! – Man, I suck at this.

1 cup frozen lima beans- My friend is trying to be a stand up comedian. This is his material. He goes: *Can February March? No, but April May.* I told him not to quit his job. Do you agree?

1 cup frozen baby carrots- Fun story… I was at the tanning salon, and I hear these two girls arguing… One of the girl's daughter runs up to the other lady and yells *"Shut the F*ck up CARROT."*

1 cup frozen yellow sweet corn- Yesterday, I accidentally swallowed some food coloring. The doctor says I'm okay, but I feel like I've dyed a little inside.

2 tablespoons chopped onions- My friend goes… *My wallet is like onion. Whenever I open it, I cry.* I relate man!

1 tablespoon OLD BAY® Seasoning- I wonder what your OLD BAAAYY would say about this. Honestly screw that donkey.

1 pound lump crabmeat- My friend is jewish, very nice lad. He goes: *How does Moses make coffee? He-brews it.*

Do This:

I DO NOT think that you are ready! This is honestly the quickest recipe I ever saw. You are welcome!

Step Number UNO!

PLACE all ingredients, except crabmeat, in 4-quart saucepan.

Step Numero DOS!

BRING to boil on medium heat. Reduce heat to low; cover and simmer 5 minutes.

STEP THREE!

STIR in crabmeat; cover and simmer 10 minutes.

I told you... This is ridiculously easy!

__Disclaimer:__ Anyone can cook this! If you nailed this congratulations! Fun fact: My sister speaks 3 languages fluently! Polish, Spanish and English. Hence why I used Spanish in this. Why only two words? Well that is how much I know. Im kidding *DIOS MIOS!*

Brown sugar bourbon grill explosion!
in case you do not own a grill works for the oven too!

About the dish:

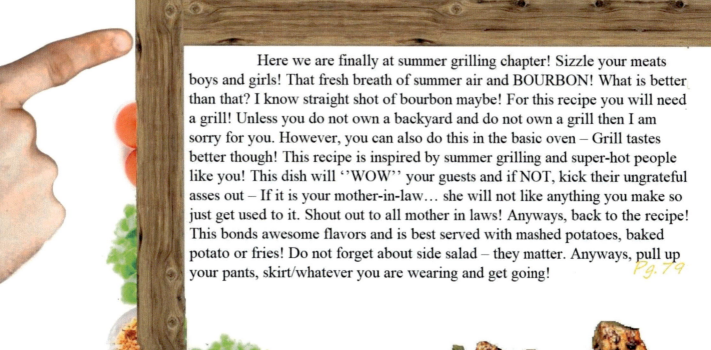

Here we are finally at summer grilling chapter! Sizzle your meats boys and girls! That fresh breath of summer air and BOURBON! What is better than that? I know straight shot of bourbon maybe! For this recipe you will need a grill! Unless you do not own a backyard and do not own a grill then I am sorry for you. However, you can also do this in the basic oven – Grill tastes better though! This recipe is inspired by summer grilling and super-hot people like you! This dish will ''WOW'' your guests and if NOT, kick their ungrateful asses out – If it is your mother-in-law… she will not like anything you make so just get used to it. Shout out to all mother in laws! Anyways, back to the recipe! This bonds awesome flavors and is best served with mashed potatoes, baked potato or fries! Do not forget about side salad – they matter. Anyways, pull up your pants, skirt/whatever you are wearing and get going!

Serving: 4-5 People, 7 Dogs and 0 Orcas.
Prep Time: 30-60 minutes. WAIT do not get discouraged it is because marinade takes time. I did not MAKE THE RULES. I mean I did but whatever!
Cook Time: 15 Mins. Give or take. Don't BURN IT!

Get This:

3 Big Chicken breasts (or any boneless chicken you have!)

5 Cloves of garlic - #DadJokeOfTheDay - My girlfriend told me to kiss her where it stinks.....So I drove her to New Jersey. (I personally love New Jersey!)

1 Large onion: What is that smell? Its not the onion… you my dear might need a TIC TAC!

1 package of mushrooms (medium size): #AnotherDadJokeOfTheDay: What do you call a book about mushrooms? A fun-guide.

1 package of brown sugar bourbon marinade mix (most grocery stores have them) – or if you are not lazy. We can make one from scratch! You will need: ½ cup bourbon, ⅓ cup brown sugar, ¼ cup balsamic vinegar, 2 tablespoons olive oil, 1 tablespoon whole grain mustard, 3 cloves garlic, finely chopped or grated, 1 teaspoon dried rosemary and pinch crushed red pepper flakes.

IF YOU CHOSE TO MAKE YOUR OWN MARINADE FROM SCRATCH WITH INGREDIENTS LISTED ABOVE DO NOT GET THESE INGREDIENTS BELOW – FOLLOW INGREDIENT REQUIREMENTS ABOVE INSTEAD.

1/4 cup of oil... You know the drill any oil your little soul desires! Also, funny part time... I asked my grandpa once, *"after 65 years you still call grandma darling, beautiful, and honey. What's your secret?"* Grandpa then responded, *"I forgot her name 5 years ago, I'm too scared to ask her."*

2TBS of water - Good life tip, if you become seriously depressed, try drinking a gallon of water, before you go to bed. - That will give you a reason to get out of bed in the morning. Told you it is a good tip! Works every time!

1TBS of vinegar - My friend Charles goes *''My girlfriend said she wanted to experiment more in the bedroom... I don't know why she got so mad when I put my baking soda and vinegar volcano next to the nightstand.''* Do not take tips from Charles. He's now single.

Do This:

BEFORE we move to the grill, cut onions into smaller slices, do the same with mushrooms. Take out a pan, add some oil and fry for 5 minutes until tender. Add two gloves of minced garlic in the last 30 seconds of frying. SET ASIDE.

TAKE the package of brown sugar bourbon marinade and mix with oil, vinegar, water and minced garlic into a bowl. Stir all together in a bowl.

If you chose to make your own marinade from scratch do this instead: Add bourbon, brown sugar, balsamic vinegar, olive oil, mustard, garlic, rosemary, & crushed red pepper flakes, if using, to a bowl or jar. Season with 2 teaspoons kosher salt & ground black pepper to taste. Whisk, mix or shake to combine.

CUT the breasts into decent size cuts, I cut one large breast into 2 decent pieces. Make sure you get a bigger bowl. Place chicken in the bowl, drop marinade into the same bowl. Cover up and refrigerate for 30-60 minutes. FUN TIP: Stab (Just the chicken don't look at your hubby he done nothing!) the breast with fork to make little holes. Therefore, marinade can enter deeper. That is what she said!

ONCE it is done, take it out of the fridge (obviously) and turn on a grill (you know outside BBQ). Put it on medium and let the breast grill until cooked. (6-8 minutes each side depends on the size of your chicken cut). Make sure you flip it. You will have marinade left in the bowl. Take a brush and keep adding it into the chicken time and again while cooking. Once it is done, pair it with some mashed potatoes, baked potato or fries (calories what? If you eat like a whale *cough, cough ME* definitely pair with mash potatoes)! #AnothetFunFact you can find mash potato recipe somewhere in the book. Also, can pair it with a salad or an ICE cube if you're on diet ha-ha.

ONCE chicken is done, transfer it to a platter and cover it with onions and mushrooms you fried earlier. Serve with side of mash potatoes!

Quick home-made bacon mash potatoes 4 large potatoes, ½ cup of cream cheese, 4 tablespoons of milk, 2 tablespoons of butter, ½ cup of finely chopped parsley, 6 slices of bacon fried and crushed. *Directions:* Peel 4 potatoes, cut them into small pieces, boil in the water for about 10-15 minutes (depends on the size of the potato cut) once boiled, mash the potatoes add cream cheese, milk, butter, parsley and crushed bacon. Season to taste with pepper and salt. If you want more creamy potatoes keep adding more milk.

Disclaimer: If you do not have a grill, I am not sure if it will taste as good from the oven. Try it on your own terms. Do not blame me if it does not. STOP... Thanks Bye*

I am putting you on spot.
TAKE THE DAMN SHOT NOW

← If you are underage. Get a juice box instead.

Pg. 81

Grilled Steak (Livin' La Vida Loca)
Because why not!

About the dish:

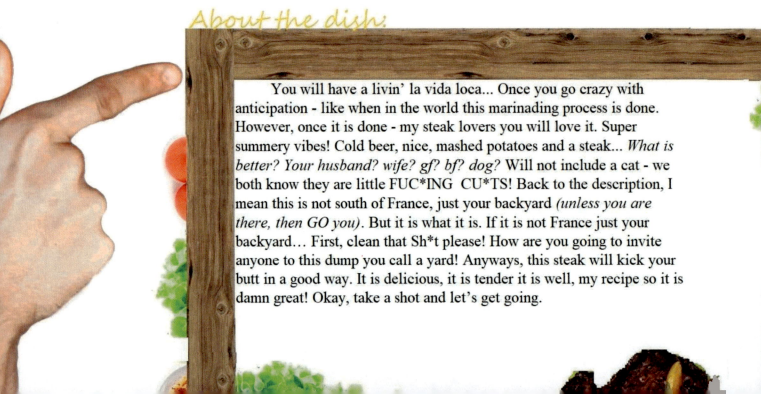

You will have a livin' la vida loca... Once you go crazy with anticipation - like when in the world this marinading process is done. However, once it is done - my steak lovers you will love it. Super summery vibes! Cold beer, nice, mashed potatoes and a steak... *What is better? Your husband? wife? gf? bf? dog?* Will not include a cat - we both know they are little FUC*ING CU*TS! Back to the description, I mean this is not south of France, just your backyard *(unless you are there, then GO you)*. But it is what it is. If it is not France just your backyard… First, clean that Sh*t please! How are you going to invite anyone to this dump you call a yard! Anyways, this steak will kick your butt in a good way. It is delicious, it is tender it is well, my recipe so it is damn great! Okay, take a shot and let's get going.

Servings: 4 humans, 1 dog, absolutely no cats!

Prep Time: 12 hours ... Okay hear me out, 12 hours or more is for marinading. Therefore, if you have an upcoming cook out do this day before. I know it is long… But it is a steak! Bit*h takes time!

Cook Time: 10 minutes more or less!

Get This:

4 1-inch-thick steaks of choice (ribeye, strip, sirloin, etc.), about 1 1/2 pounds - Choose well!

2 lemons, zested - You do not know how to zest a lemon?... Go online. Research! What am I Uncle GOOOOGLE?

6 tablespoons olive oil - Or any oil really. I say that in all recipes. Because if you do not have olive oil, you will not ruin this with a different kind.

8 sprigs fresh rosemary, broken in half - Kind of like you. Cheer up. If nothing goes straight, go gay.

2 teaspoon ground black pepper - #DadJokeOfTheDay - Why did Pepper go to prison? FOR - A-SALT....

12 garlic cloves - Grated or crushed - Well, this is about to smell interesting.

2 tablespoon dried oregano - So my neighbor kid goes: *Roses are red. Your blood is too. You look like a monkey and belong in a zoo. Do not worry, I'll be there too. Not in the cage, but laughing at you.* Okay you little Fu*king prick.......

4 teaspoons crushed red pepper flakes - Crushed, kind of like my heart now. After you keep roasting my book, while looking at my face. Damn JOE!

4 teaspoons Kosher salt – A truly salty story! A driving teacher asks his student "There are 2 people standing on the road, your mother-in-law and your wife. What do you hit?" *Student:* "My mother-in-law" *Teacher:* "For the 3rd time Harry, you'll hit the brakes damn it!"

Pg. 83

Do This:

ADD the steaks to an airtight container or bowl. Top with the olive oil, lemon zest, garlic, fresh (Fresh that was you 10 years ago, that's some scary sh*t) Rosemary sprigs, dried (Dried - That's you now, sadly) Oregano, crushed red pepper flake, & ground black pepper. (Please do not season the steaks with salt!) Rub the herbs & spices into all surfaces of the steaks (Do it the way you want your lover to rub you! ha-ha! Passion Linda, passion). Cover and transfer to the refrigerator. Marinate for at least 12 hours. More is fine as well.

TURN on the grill! Tastes good if you get buy a wood plank! And lay the steak on top of it while grilling. Adds a lot FANCY, to the steak.

ABOUT 25 minutes prior to grilling the steaks, pull them out of the refrigerator - Let them come up to room temperature. Steak will grill more evenly at room temperature vs cold, so it is important to give it a little time to warm up! Just before tossing them on the grill, use paper towel, pat the steak as dry, then season generously with Kosher salt. You know funny story to some *Please do not get offended* Once my grandpa invited a vegan friend over BBQ. He goes... Listen Dan there's that moment when you put your steak on the grill and your mouth waters all over from that amazing smell... Dan, do you vegans feel the same when you mow the grass? .. *Me stares in the distance nearly choking on my damn spoon*

PLACE the steak over direct medium heat (Is this what hell feels like?). Grill 2-3 minutes per side for a medium rare, until a meat thermometer inserted in the center of the steak shows 140F. If needed more time add 1 extra minute of grill time per side for 1 extra level of doneness. If you use the wood plank, the time will be little longer. It will be medium rare on the wood plank as well once it reaches 140F in the center of each steak.

SET aside to rest for 4-8 minutes before slicing and serving.

Serve with bacon mash potatoes from the SIDES chapter of the book. Or do whatever the heck you want!

<u>Disclaimer:</u> Vegan joke was not meant to insult anyone, apologies if they did. My grandpa is a savage...Cannot take him anywhere

My face each time you fu*k up!

Was this hard?

YES	NO
Sadly you selected this option. This option offers no reward. K Bye.	Congrats for being a pro. You deserve a milion dollars. However, I do not have it. So your reward is a shot. Which also you have to serve yourself

Avocado Glazed Salmon

Straight of your grill! your mom likes it, at least that's what she told me.

About the dish:

This is a great recipe for a healthy summer dish straight from the grill. Paired with rice, wine and it is like you are on *Mediterranean Sea* coast. Then you get reality check, and you are eating this in your ...crappy smelly backyard. Well, I mean this is a great light recipe either or! Let the summer begin. We had chicken, we had steak now it's time for salmon! The flavors in this dish will rock your body, knock socks off your guests and make the party great again! *Let this recipe begin!*

Pg.85

Serving: 4 humans, no dogs maybe a cat.

Prep time: 35 minutes - It is long because you need to marinade this Mary-Ann!

Cook Time: 6 minutes - Unless you got some chunky as salmon...

Get This:

1 tablespoon olive oil - Or any oil you have. I'm not here to judge you, Judy.

1 teaspoon salt - Kind of like your personality. Half spoon of sugar sweet, and 1 teaspoon of fuc**ng salty a*s.

1 teaspoon pepper - This has nothing to do with this ingredient, but I just remembered this joke. What do you call a singing laptop? A-DELL! Please do not cancel me.

1 teaspoon paprika - I used to know this guy, his name was.... Drum roll... PEPE RIKKA... It is a true story. His parents must love peppers! Thank you. Bye.

4 salmon fillets - People say smoking will give you diseases. What they do not know is that it cures salmon. Mic Drop.

2 avocados - #DadJokeOfTheDay - *Prepare for this* - You cannot judge any avocado until you guac-a-mile in his shoes. Mhmm... I get it. I am so lame.

¼ red onion - The other day my friend told me he had the body of a Greek god. I had to explain to him that Buddha is not Greek.

1 lime, juiced - Yesterday my friend's wife got him upset, he said: *I was today years old when I realized I didn't like you.* She replied: *Someday you'll go far, and I really hope you stay there.* Then he said: *Oops, my bad. I could've sworn I was dealing with an adult.* She cringed and said: *I've been called worse things by better men. How many licks until I get to the interesting part of this conversation?* He ended with: *I'll never forget the first time we met. But I'll keep trying.* She nodded: *Who are you sir? And what are you doing in my house.*

1 ½ teaspoons salt - I was at McD's today and this older lady stood up and went towards this insanely loud crying kid's mom and said: *Your kid is so fu*king annoying, he makes my Happy Meal cry.*

OPTIONAL: cilantro, chopped for garnish

Do This:

IN a large bowl, mix oil, salt, pepper, and paprika. Coat the salmon fillets with the marinade and refrigerate for 30 minutes. Do it. Do not cut the time. At least something is marinading at your house. Cannot say the same thing about your romantic life. Ooops. I did it again.

GRILL the salmon on an 11-inch (28 cm) griddle pan on high heat for three minutes on each side. Trying to be healthy here.

IN a separate bowl, lightly squishy squish avocados, ¼ red onion with a fork, the juice from one lime, 1 tablespoon olive oil, and salt to taste.

SPOON avocado salsa on top of the cooked salmon. Top with finely cut cilantro. Pairs well with rice! Or simply asparagus!

QUICK ASPARAGUS RECIPE ADD ON: Get asparagus, dump it on the pan, add some oil. Put on medium. Add pinch salt, pepper & red pepper flakes to taste. Cover and let it cook for 6 minutes. Flip it around a bit *(stop winking at your lover. You look like something got into your damn Fuc**ng eye Linda.)* Once its soft, add fresh minced garlic and add panko breadcrumbs. Fry for another 2 minutes. Voila!

Disclaimer: I will not lie; this pairs well with wine. Any wine! On a beautiful summer day. Unless you live in England... It rains... Fuc**ng rains... all the damn time. Shoutout to the UK

Crossword- if you complete you deserve a shot if not then all you get is water.

1. Another word for stupid? No it is not your spouse!
2. Which country invented VODKA?
3. Name of the author of this amazing book.
4. _____ cube.
5. What gets laid more often than you?
    You said it not me ^

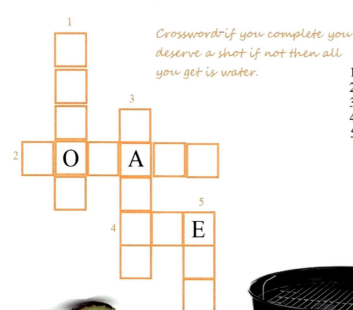

Super Loaded Baked Summer Potatoes from the grill!
What a long name.

About the dish:

Well, this such a summery side dish that pairs amazing with steak, ribs basically anything. It was a random recipe that just appeared to me in a dream... Yeah total Bull Sh*t from my part... I just made it one day with whatever I had around and was not bad at all. It is quite tasty. Taste like a dish you get on that nice summer night camping with loved ones, or alone with cats. It is great for BBQ parties, this and that blah blah.... If you need more than 5 servings just multiply everything by 2 to make 10 servings. If you do not know math. Sorry to say... Make the recipe twice? ha-ha. Okay let's go!

Serving: 5 perhaps...
Prep Time: 10 minutes. Depends how clumsy you are!
Cook Time: 30 minutes.

Before you make this happen sign this waiver first.

_____ - sign this waver in case my dumb ass burns myself, sets my house on fire, or damage the top of my outdoor table. I will not sue the creator of this book *(he's awesome!)*. I am the dummy responsible of casualties, burns and broken furniture. If not signed, do not do this recipe – as I will hunt you in your dreams. K bye.

Get This:

1 bag of baby potatoes - If you ever want to see a human potato.... Look at the cover of this book. Thank you. Mic drops.

1 1/2 cup of parmesan cheese - Totally love parmesan. Who does not! It sorts of smells like my neighbor Rick though. Hi Rick!

1/4 cup of FRESH parsley - My grandpa goes: *What did the ranch say when somebody opened the refrigerator? "Hey, close the door! I'm dressing!"* You guessed he is not a comedian.

2 cups of fried crushed bacon - This totally adds to this dish so make sure you do not skip this! Like you skip that gym you signed up 2 years ago Carol.

2 cups of Sour cream - #DadJokeOfTheDay - I heard the government was putting chips in people. Well, mine better be sour cream and onion. Okay ill see me out. Bye. *Slams doors*

1/4 cup of oil - My friend's wife asked her husband, *"What do you like most in me, my pretty face or my sexy body?"* He looked at her from head to toe and replied, *"I like your sense of humor!"*

1/4 cup of butter – Preferably salty, like your soul.

2 gloves of garlic - Mince the hell out of it. Rest in peace garlic, you will be minced!

salt and pepper – to taste like usual.

Do This:

GET a baking pan that will fit inside your grill. Put oil and butter inside. Drop the babies in. *(Cheesus... not your babies I know they are pain in the a*s crack, but I was talking about potatoes!)* add salt and hefty amount of pepper. Set your grill on medium. Once the potatoes become soft *(20-25 minutes)*, add minced garlic, only 1 cup of parsley and parmesan cheese, mix it with a spoon. Please be careful you clumsy bum.

LET it bake for 3-5 minutes more. Once the potatoes fully bake *BE CAREFUL THE BAKING PAN WILL BE EXTREMLY HOT YOU CAN'T AFFORD ANY ACCIDENTS WITH THAT CRAPPY INSURANCE YOU'VE GOT* Transfer them lovely potatoes into a non-plastic bowl. Add sour cream, bacon and remaining fresh parsley, mix. Add more salt and pepper if needed.

Disclaimer: I am not responsible for your clumsy a*s if you burn your damn finger. Thanks, bye. *

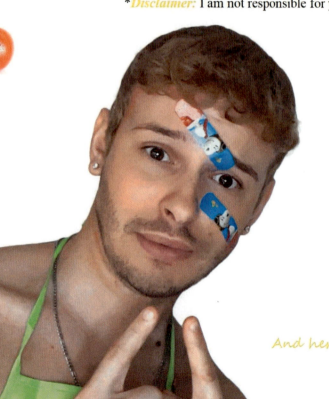

If your dumb*as ended up looking like this. Here is a bandage

CLUMSY ALERT

And here is a shot to make it better!

The Burgerzilla!
Can be done on the stove or on the grill!

About the dish:

Honestly, this is my staple recipe. This burger is literally to die for *(please do not die!)*. So many rich flavors as well as home-made hamburger sauce! This will knock not only shoes but socks off your guests! If you cannot cook for sh*t… then try this… it is easy! It will make you look like the 5-star chef you are… or aspire to be… *You cannot cook? Have two left hands?* Well, this recipe is just for you. Wow - yourself into getting laid after making this. I am sure your mother-in-law will finally compliment you for once after making this hamburger… If not do not invite her next time. This pairs well with BEER! Or soft drink of your choice! Side fries anyone? Hell-YES! Okay, let's go!

Serving: 6 patties!
Prep Time: 10 minutes! Unless you are super clumsy.
Cook Time: 8-10 minutes!

Get This:

Condiments: 6 buns, hamburger pickles, cheese slices, lettuce, onion rings, tomato.

FOR THE PATTIES: *2 pounds ground meat (turkey/beef)* – This lady at Mc D's was eating her food next to a super loud annoying kid. She got up to the kiddo's mother and said: *Your kid is so fuc*king annoying she made my happy meal cry.*

1 cup cheese flavor or Panko breadcrumbs – A blonde drops off her dress to the dry cleaners. The lady says, *"Come Again!"*. The blonde says, *"No, it's toothpaste this time."* It is what it is!

1 large egg – #DadJokeOfTheDay - I couldn't figure out why the baseball kept getting larger. Then it hit me.

1 teaspoon salt – This kid next to me fought with another one, then yelled: *Yo mama so fat, she doesn't need internet, she's already worldwide.*

3TBS of pickle juice (from hamburger chips jar) – Everyone knows a weird kid from school, in my case this kid at my old High-School used to fart a lot. Everytime he ever fart in public, he yell, *"Turbo power!"* and walked faster.

2 teaspoon garlic powder – Interviewer: *"What's your greatest weakness?"* Me: *"Honesty."* Interviewer: *"I don't think honesty is a weakness."* Me: *"I don't give a f*ck what you think."* See what I did there.

2 teaspoon onion powder – Onion makes you cry. So did your EX.

1 teaspoon black pepper – I hope you own spoons.

For sauce:

1 cup of BBQ – Any sauce. Seriously whichever one you fancy!

2 cups of mayo – Light travels faster than sound. This is why some people appear bright until you hear them speak.

3TBS of pickle juice – From hamburger chips.

2TBS of garlic powder – Get the best brand!

1 Spoon of mustard – You can add more to your liking.

Do This:

SET out a large mixing bowl. Add in the ground turkey/beef, and every ingredient from the pattie section. Mix by hand until the meat mixture is very smooth.

PRESS the meat down in the bowl, into an even disk. Use a knife to cut and divide the hamburger patty mixture into *6-1/3 pound grill or skillet patties, or 12 thin griddle patties.*

If using a grill:

SHAPE a pattie - size to your liking. Set on a gril. Preheat the grill. Cook for 3-2 minutes each side. In the last flip add cheese.

If using an oven:

SET out a baking sheet, lined with wax paper or foil, to hold the patties. One at a time, gather the patty mix and press firmly into patties. Shape them just slightly larger than the buns you plan to use, to account for shrinkage during cooking. Set the patties on the baking sheet. Use a spoon to press a dent in the center of each patty so they don't puff up as they cook. If you need to stack the patties separate them with a sheet of wax paper. Preheat oil on a skillet on medium/high. Fry for about 3 to 4 minutes per side. In the last flip. Add cheese wait until it melts.

For thick patties: GRILL or fry the patties for 3-4 minutes per side.

For thin patties: COOK on the griddle for 2 minutes per side.

For the sauce: MIX all the ingredients in a bowl until smooth.

Serve: Add *1 TBS* of sauce on the bun, then place lettuce and tomato, add pattie, then add another *1TBS* of sauce, at the end add onion rings and hamburger chips.

You did it. You deserve this!

"Welcome To Grandma"

About her:

Teresa Ogonowska – My lovely grandmother. She is always the first one to dance! No KIDDING! Women in my family live super long and stay young for super long! Good genes! She has a super kind heart not only to her kids but grandkids and prepare…. Grand, grand kids as well!

She is loving, kind and giving. She could give her last piece of bread to a stranger if she seen them in need. Her hospitality deserves an A+! Therefore, I wanted to include her in this book as well. She will present to you her pick of 3 traditional dishes in this chapter. *Let's cook!*

Kotlety Mielone *Don't even try to pronounce it*
(think about meatballs but more oval and bigger without tomato sauce!) They are awesome!

About the dish:

This is truly my grandmother's favorite meat dish. If done right its delicious. So dont F*** it up yall!. Also, any leftovers can be used in a sandwich! It is even yummier that way! Pair it with lettuce, onions and some mayo or dressing and awesome sandwich is born. I mean grandma knows best. My wonderful grandmother Teresa *(Theresa in English)* cooks all the time.. My grandpa is a lucky lad.. Ehhh.. You can tell just by looking at him that he is well FED. Anyways, give this one a go. Pair it as a dinner with mash potatoes & salad, or as a toasted sandwich with lettuce, onion, tomato, cucumber and dressing! Little backstory! They are one of the most popular meals in Poland, where they are known as "kotlety mielone". *(Pron.CO-Thle-ty Myeh - LOH-neh)*. It dates to 1706. Was a popular dish among polish royals. See, you learn how to cook, learn some language and some history! How informative is this book! Okay let's get going!

Serving: 4 could be 5 honestly or more depends how little or how much you eat!

Prep time: 10 Minutes unless you need more. Shots anyone? You might need one for this!

Cook time: 20-25 minutes!

Get This:

1Lbs of (Either Pork, Chicken, or Turkey - You can also mix 2! WHY NOT EXPERIMENT!

1 Egg <---- #DadJokeOfTheDay – What is the difference between you and an EGG? EGGS get laid, you however do not.

1 Onion - I saw a young teenage kid on the subway today. He had a Mohawk hairstyle dyed yellow, green, and red. He caught me staring at him and in a nasty voice asked, *"What the f*ck are you looking at?"* I replied, *"Sorry, but when I was about your age I had sex with a parrot. I thought maybe you were my son."* A Parrot really David! Under preassure that was the best I could come up with.

3 Cloves of garlic minced - Rest in peace, garlic --You will be minced! Funny story my friend's mom said to her son: *"You born on the highway"* Jerry: *"Uh no, I was not.."* Her: *"You were, because that's where most accidents happen."* She was clealry mad at him for something. His face was priceless.

3 Tablespoons of breadcrumbs PLAIN *(just like your dating life)* – However, you can use some flavored breadcrumbs.

1 teaspoon of pepper, marjoram, & salt. - My friend's kid does not like his neighbor. She always yells at him for literally no reason. So finally he had enough and walked up to her and said: *If beauty was a drop of water, you'd be the Sahara Desert.* Her confused: *Get out of my lawn.* He then sat on the lawn and said: *Listen Pam, are you always this stupid or are you just making a special effort today?*

Now take a sip of a drink with my grandmother! NA-ZDROWIE – that is cheers in Polish.

NA ZDROWIE - (pron. Na-Zdro-vie)

Do This:

TAKE another shot! or two... ehh vodka goes well with this dish! BOTTOMS UP *looks over at your husband* What is a polish dish with no VODKA!

MIX all the ingredients in a bowl, including the meat and egg. Mix it together, squeeze it, spank it GIVE IT SOME LOVE REBECCA! Now the fun part! ... Well make a meatball but larger one... instead of ball make it an oval about 3-4'' long and make the sides little flatter around 1''. Kind of like a patty but thick (oh she's sassy).

NOW the fun part. Get yourself a pan! add 1/2 cup of oil, Any oil really! Who cares...? I do not... set the heat to medium and warm up the oil. Sizzle Baby! Now take the Misshaped ovals and roll them again in breadcrumbs! Now carefully put it on the pan! Cook each side 5-6 minutes! DON'T BURN IT! – Get it like the tittle! Ha-ha. Cover with lid for faster cooking. MAKE SURE TO CHECK if it's cooked thru, I don't know how big balls you made! Fry until JUICES run clear... (yours ran clear years ago... is that sand ?!?!)

PAIR with mash potatoes and any salad! Great for dinner!

Disclaimer: *You are slowly turning into an alcoholic... Do not blame me...*

Quick home-made bacon mash potatoes

4 large potatoes, ½ cup of cream cheese, 4 tablespoons of milk, 2 tablespoons of butter, ½ cup of finely chopped parsley, 6 slices of bacon fried and crushed. Directions: Peel 4 potatoes, cut them into small pieces, boil in the water for about 10-15 minutes *(depends on the size of the potato cut)* once boiled, mash the potatoes add cream cheese, milk, butter, parsley and crushed bacon. Season to taste with pepper and salt. If you want more creamy potatoes keep adding more milk.

Additionally, pair with a red cabbage salad – thank me later! You can find this recipe in the chapter dedicated to my sister. Also, you can make a toast sandwich, cut the kotlety in half and put it on top of the toast with lettuce, cheese, tomato and cucumber. Drop your favorite dressing on top. VOILA!

Pg. 97

Authentic Polish Pierogi with meat
Not that BS kind

About the dish:

There are many, many kinds of pierogies out there, savory ones and sweet ones. This is another take on pierogies… This time with meat! If you have not tried a truly authentic version yet, then definitely give these a-go. These are the real deal straight off a pole. (Not a stripper's pole... Pole is what a Polish person is named in English language you non cultured specimen). It always makes me laugh when people mispronounce this dish. Pirogi, Perogis, Peregis... I think I have heard all different types by now, CUT THAT SHI*. International lesson #1 - Put that wine glass down and pay damn attention. It is pronounced "pih-eh-ro-ge". Okay? Got it? Perfect! Let us move on. To make this dish, you need patience ... If you do not have patience, take 2 shots and your perception shall change. Unless you are an angry drinker than a half-folded pierogi might fly thru the kitchen. Oh well. Let us go! Remember grandma is watching!

Servings: About 50 pierogies. Do not worry you can freeze them for later! They last long in the freezer.
Prep Time: around 40 minutes.
Cook Time: 15-20 minutes.

Get This:

For The Filling:

1.5 lb (600-700 g) cooked meat, ideally beef, but also poultry, turkey will work too – Get the best meat possible.

1 (approx. 3.8 oz, 110 g) white onion – I would of tell you a joke, but it is hard to cry and laugh at the same time!

1 tsp salt – My older freind said: Don't worry, the first 40 years of childhood are always the hardest.

For Topping:

2 tbsp butter – I want to tell you a butter joke…However, you will spread it.

1 short link (3 oz, 90 g) Polish kietbasa sausage – My friend once said this to her husband: *When you look in the mirror, say hi to the clown you see in there for me, would you?* He replied: *I don't have to. I wake up next to one daily.* R.I.P Charles.

1/2 fine chopped onion - I remember when you were described as FINE... What happened? ... Seriously though!

2 tbsp chives, chopped - #DadJokeOfTheDay - My waiter asked, "would you like sour cream, bacon and chives on your potato?" my response…"That's a loaded question...

For The Dough:

2 cups (500 g) all-purpose flour – Totally unrelated but funny. My grandpa goes… *What is the true purpose of Valentine's Day?* Me: *What?* Him: *To remind single people that they are single.*

1 cup (8.45 fl oz, 250 ml) hot water – I was at the restaurant with friend's family. His dad said to his mother: *Hey, you have something on your chin.* Her: *here?* Him: *No, the 3rd one down.* Ouch.

1 tsp salt - I believed in evolution until I met you.

Pg. 99

Do This:

Filling: **GRIND** the meat in a meat grinder or use a food processor/blender instead.

PEEL and chop the onion finely. Chop, chop, chop Becky! Add some oil to the frying pan, wait for it to warm up. Add the chopped onion and fry until golden.

SEASON meat with pepper and salt. Fry until almost cooked. 5 minutes.

ADD fried onion to the meat. Season well with salt and pepper. Have a try - does it need more spice? If so, add some garlic powder or smoked paprika powder. Blend well with a spoon or a spatula.

IF the filling appears too dry, add a few spoons of water or broth - meat should be sticky.

For The Dough: **PREPARE** a clean work surface. Clean, clean, clean Cinderella! Sift the flour, make a small well. Pour in a few spoonful of hot water.

KNEAD flour and water together. Gradually add more water, until the dough becomes elastic and soft. Like your skin ages ago.

DIVIDE the dough into four parts. Spread one part on the work surface, roll into a thin layer of dough. Use a glass to cut out decent size circles.

PLACE a spoonful of meat filling in the middle. Fold dough over filling. Press edges together.

CONTINUE forming until all pierogi are assembled

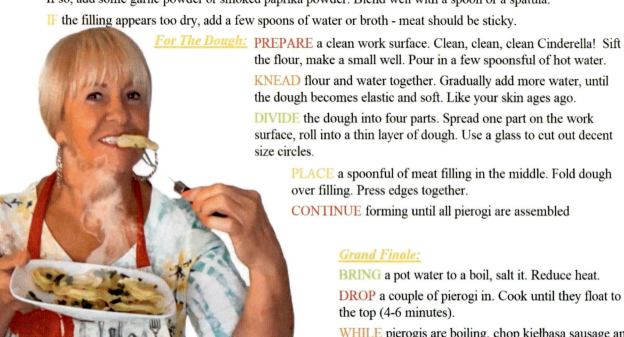

Grand Finale:

BRING a pot water to a boil, salt it. Reduce heat.

DROP a couple of pierogi in. Cook until they float to the top (4-6 minutes).

WHILE pierogis are boiling, chop kiełbasa sausage and 1/2 onion into cubes. Melt 2 tablespoons of butter on a frying pan, drop in kiełbasa and onions, let them fry until golden. If using bacon, use 6 slices, fry until crisp, wait till it will cool down – then crush.

COLLECT the dumplings with a slotted spoon.

SERVE pierogi, topping them with melted butter and fried onion/kiełbasa pieces. (Or bacon) Sprinkle with chopped chives.

CONTINUE TO THE NEXT PAGE

CONTINUATION:

Try fried version:

COMPLETE all the steps. Once pierogies are boiled. Let them cool down. Once they cool down, add some oil to the pain and fry until golden brown (4-5 minutes each side). Once done add some sour cream on top, crushed bacon and fresh parsley. Season to taste with pepper and salt!

Try both!

F R I E D

B O I L E D

Disclaimer: My grandma was watching your steps. She is proud to say you did not fuc this up! Congrats. For the ones who did not do this recipe justice. Mt grandma says: *TRY AGAIN!* *

Game Challenge! You must complete!

Directions:

Drink 1 shot liquour of choice. Do 10 push ups.
⇧
Skip push ups. However, increase the shot dosage to 2.

Pick one of the cards. You must pick one. You must follow the steps on them. If you do not, this dish will give you diarrhea. Also, don't be boring play the damn game.

Take 1 shot of hot sauce. Yell "I'm a chicken"..
⇧
That is what you get for not wanting a shot of liquour.

Schabowe Dinner!
Polish pork chops

About the dish:

This is a recipe for Schabowe - full dinner! Schabowe (pron. S-ha-Bo-vee) is a traditional polish dish originated in Poland between year 1850-1860. Was formally a dish reserved for higher status Szlachta (polish royals, dukes, etc.)? This is an extremely popular dinner dish in Poland. I grew up eating this and I must say as much as I am not a fan of pork – I never turned down this dish. My grandma and my whole family make it for holidays and usually for dinners time to time. It is best served with sauerkraut and mash potatoes! This recipe however we will skip sauerkraut. As it is super time consuming. If you ever find it at any European deli buy it and serve as a side. This dish, we will pair with fried brussels sprouts and mash potatoes. Do not worry you will not need to switch between pages to find recipes for the sides as I will include it in this recipe for time saving and for you – so you cannot fu*k up the pages with your dirty hands! Okay, take a deep breath or a shot! Let's go!

Servings: 4 adults.
Prep Time: 15 minutes.
Cook Time: All together around 30 minutes perhaps.

Get This:

For Schabowe (Pork Chop):

4 boneless pork chops - #DadJokeOfTheDay - *What's green and smells like pork?* - Kermit's finger. Get it?

1 tablespoon all-purpose flour - #AnotherDadJokeOfTheDay - *What kind of flour should you use to make a cake for a cat?* - All purr-puss flour. Oh, I'm so lame!

1 egg – My neighbor Chuck tries to be a stand-up comedian. Therefore, he wanted to present me with his material. Chuck goes: *What does a meditating egg say?* Me: *What does it say Chuck?* He goes: *Ohmmmmmmmlet!!!!!* Dear Chuck, do not quit your day job.

5 tablespoons breadcrumbs – I will be professional here. You can either use plain one or flavored. Sky is the limit kid!

2 tablespoons vegetable oil, or as needed – My friend pis*sed off his wife, she said : *You should carry a plant around with you to replace the oxygen you waste.* Then she added: *If you were the light at the end of the tunnel, I'd turn back around.* She did not play.

salt and freshly ground black pepper to taste.

For dill potatoes:

1 lb baby potatoes - My grandma goes… *Have you ever seen a human potato?* If not, tell grandpa to send you a selfie. Ouch.

1 tbsp Butter - #AnotherDadJokeOfTheDay - Don't ask me to tell you that joke about butter. I refuse to spread it. I know I cannot be a comedian.

1 tbsp Sour Cream (or Cream Cheese) – My friend goes: All of my relationships experiences are inside Sour Patch Kids bag. Sweet, sour, fuc*ing gone. Do you relate?

Fresh Dill - What's pickle's favorite game show? Let's Make a Dill!! Okay well I tried an original joke. I failed!

Ingredients for another side - next page!

CONTINUATION:

For Brussels Sprouts:

2 teaspoons crushed garlic- These two teenagers were arguing next to me in line. One went: *I will slap you so hard even Google won't be able to find you.* The other replied: *I have seen people like you. But I had to pay admission.* I was just standing there sipping my soda and waited for hell to break lose.

¼ white onion, chopped- You know funny story to some *Please do not get offended* Once my grandpa invited a vegan friend over BBQ. He goes... Listen Dan there is that moment when you put your steak on the grill and your mouth waters all over from that amazing smell... Dan, do you vegans feel the same when you mow the grass? ... *Me stares in the distance nearly choking on my fuck*ng spoon*

1 (16 ounce) package trimmed Brussels sprouts- Totally offensive and bad joke from my neighbor Chuck! Here it goes. What do you call a hooker's kid? A brothel sprout... See this is why Chuck kept his day job.

2 cloves of garlic- I was sitting in a bar one day and two really large women came in, talking in an interesting accent. So I said, *"Cool accent, are you two ladies from Ireland?"* One of them snarled at me, *"It's Wales, Dumbo!"* I was no longer nice as she was super bitter, so I corrected myself, *"My apologies, so are you two whales from Ireland?"* We all ended up eating together. I forgot how dark Eruopean humor can be.

salt and ground black pepper to taste.

Continue to the next page!

Oucick polish salad (if you want to add it to your sides).

Mizeria (Cucumber salad):

- 1   Cucumber (medium to large size)
- ¼ cup White Vinegar
- 3 tablespoons   Sour Cream
- 2 teaspoons   Salt
- 1 teaspoon   Pepper
- add handful   Fresh Dill

How to make:

Wash and peel the cucumber. Slice into thin/medium-thin slices. Mix in bowl with vinegar, salt and pepper. Mix in the sour cream. Chop dill and add that in. Mix well and enjoy!

Enjoy

Do This:

*__Disclaimer:__ Please do not burn yourself. Emergency room is quite expensive these days! Also, do not forget to pair this dish with shot of VODKA! Na Zdrowie! (Cheers in Polish) *

Schabowe:

PLACE pork chops between 2 sheets of heavy plastic on a solid, level surface. Firmly pound *(stop giggling this is a serious business)* with the smooth side of a meat mallet, turning occasionally, until very thin. Season with salt and pepper.

NEXT, pour flour onto a large plate. Whisk egg in a wide, shallow bowl. Also, place breadcrumbs in a separate bowl. Moving on! Dredge chops with flour. Dip in whisked egg. Coat with breadcrumbs on both sides.

HEAT oil in a large skillet over medium-high heat. Add breaded chops; cook until golden brown, about 5 minutes per side. Voila! Set aside!

Dill Potatoes:

CUT baby potatoes in half. Heat up a pot of water with some salt on medium. Cut potatoes in smaller sizes. Boil until cooked thru. Usually, 8-10 minutes depends on the size. Drain. Set in a bowl on the side.

AFTER, season with salt & pepper. Then mix sour cream with dill - about half of a cup of fresh dill.

MELT butter in a microwave, and sprinkle all over potatoes (use extra spoon if needed).

SERVE with sour cream dill mixture on top. (Add more salt if needed).

Brussels Sprouts:

CUT Brussels-sprouts in half, add some oil on a medium pan. Once oil heats up on medium heat, add Brussels -season with salt & pepper to taste. Fry until bottom sides are little blackened and crispy. On separate pan, place chopped onion fry until golden. In the last 30 seconds add crushed garlic to the onions.

GET a bowl mix Brussels with onions. Season with more salt and pepper if needed. Set aside.

And just like that - you have a full dinner with two sides (technically 3 if you count cucumber salad). You learned how to cook a traditional dish, learned some language and history. You are welcome. Finally, you are 5% smarter!

Pg.105

Magical Amazing Coleslaw
(It truly is!)

About the dish:

It is terribly hard to find great coleslaw these days! Do not fear you are in the right place! This coleslaw will knock your socks off... Get you laid as well! This recipe is not hard. Quite simple. If you cannot cook for sh*t do not worry – this will not be a challenge. Little back story: The dish was initially created in the Netherlands. In fact, the term coleslaw originates from the Dutch expression koosla, which means "cabbage salad." Recipes like coleslaw have been found and used in American homes from as early as 1770. Impressive right? You would think it just recently became popular! But no! People knew this recipe in the States way before cars and planes were invented. Amazing! Well, again great lesson David! You are welcome. Get your educated butt to work. Chop, chop!

Pg.107

Serving size: 7-8 human beings.
Prep time: 10 mins
Cook time: Cook time? You mean mix time? about 3 minutes!

Get This:

1/4 shredded carrot - *(For the not so skilled ones that is about 1 medium carrot)*

2 tablespoons of minced onion - My friend thought she was soo smart, she said the only vegetable/fruit that can make her cry is a onion so I threw a coconut at her. She changed her mind real quick!!

8 cups of finely chopped cabbage - *(Usually one head)* if you wonder what size... Use your head as a reference its big enough.

1/2 cup of mayonnaise - My grandpa got upset on my uncle, so he said:

Grandpa: *"Why did the chicken cross the road?"* Uncle: *"To get to the idiot's house."*
Grandpa: *"Knock knock."* Uncle: *"Who's there?"* Grandpa: *"The chicken."*
Morale of the story: Do not fu*k around with grandpa he has been around for long time.

1/4 cup of buttermilk - My neighbor met my friend and said: *"Haven't I seen you someplace before?"* She responds, *"Yeah, that's why I don't go there anymore."*

1/4 cup of milk - Attention: Whenever your ex says, *"You'll never find someone like me,"* the answer to that is, *"That's the point."*

1/3 granulated sugar - You wish you were this sweet!

2 1/2 tablespoon of lemon juice - *(For the not so mathematical specimens walking this earth 1/2 means half)*

1 1/2 tablespoon of white vinegar - It is funny when kids argue. This kid said the following to the other kid: *Yo momma so dumb, she tried to surf the microwave.* Like how you come up with that!

1/2 teaspoon salt - #DadJokeOfTheDay - *Why are frogs always so happy?* They eat what ever bugs them. Ha-HA - NOT....

1/8 teaspoon of pepper – Grandpa goes: Some guy called me a tool when I was young. So I got hammered and nailed his girlfriend Guess he was right.

Do This:

MAKE sure cabbage and carrots are finely chopped (about the size of rice). Get your chopping skills on. Put glasses on if needed.

COMBINE sugar, mayonnaise, milk, buttermilk, lemon juice, vinegar, salt and pepper in a large bowl. Beat until its smooth. (Imagine it is your mother-in-law) Who said that... NOT ME!

NOW get that bowl out. Add cabbage, carrots and onion. Get that dressing you made into it as well. NOW STIR! MIX! When you are done - cover for 2 hours and place in refrigerator. VOILA! (uh sexy he's bilingual).

*_Disclaimer:_ Make sure it sits aside for 2 hours so all the flavors can combine. Do not cheat! Otherwise, it will be a FLOP like your outfit today. *

Game:

Draw someone you do not like. Give it a name. Laugh at it.

Then take a shot!

TACO MANIA SALAD!
(Where is tequila at?)

About the dish:

All my wonderful chefs - Dogs, cats, unicorns whatever you classify yourself as! I came out with this recipe not so long ago. I mean I am sure there is many similar ones out there. However, mine is better, thanks bye. Kidding, not about the better part. Well, it is quite wonderful for a movie night. If you like being a fat couch potato like me. Then this is for you. The flavors do combine very well. Also, what's better than taco and tequila? You have guessed! NADA! Surprise your friends on your next TACO TUESDAY or whatever day of the week you do it with this world wonder. Super easy, super-fast! Let's go!

Serving: 4 People or 1 depends on your appetite Louis.
Prep Time: 10 minutes - perhaps...
Cook Time: 15 minutes - Give or take.

Get This:

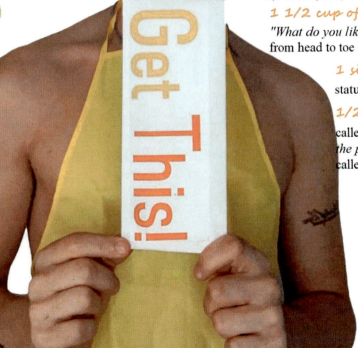

1 Lbs of either ground chicken, turkey or beef. (Choose your victim wisely).*It's just a joke all calm down*

1 package of taco seasoning - Can find it everywhere!

1 yellow onion - Time to cry some more! It is about time you invest in some tissues.

1 whole lettuce - (Romaine head, or Iceberg) - #DadJokeOfTheDay - What did lettuce said on a garden party? LETTUCE TURNIP THE BEET! Okay I know LAME. *Hides under a rock* *Please ignore me*

1 can of whole kernel corn - I was in a line next to a lady with child. She said to her son, "Look at that kid over there; he's not misbehaving." The son replied,"Maybe he has good parents then!" AWKWARDDDDD!

1 1/2 cup of shredded cheddar cheese - A husband asked his wife, "What do you like most in me, my pretty face or my sexy body?" She looked at him from head to toe and replied, "I like your sense of humor!"

1 single tomato - Single... Sorry did not mean to specify your status, Sean.

1/2 cup of sourcream -I remember when in High School some-1 called me gay.I said out *loud* so everyone could hear: *"I'm straighter than the pole your mom dances on."* I was quite a savage. Never got named called again.

1 cup of salsa - My friend's husband upset her so much she yelled across the parking lot: *Why don't you slip into something more comfortable, like a coma.* He yelled back:
*Roses are red.
Violets are blue.
I have five fingers;
The middle one's for you.*

Do This:

WHIP out that beautiful skillet of yours. Add some oil, dunk the meat of choice and fry. While its frying, mix the taco seasoning with 3 spoons of water *(Save 1 TBS of seasoning for dressing)* while you mixed the seasoning with some water. Dunk it into the meat. MIX, MIX, MIX... Fry Fry, Fry... When the meat is cooked thru. SET ASIDE.

NOW take a big bowl. Chop, chop that lettuce thin and small, follow with onion & tomato. Add whole can of corn and shredded cheddar.

FINALE now for the saucy part! Take a small bowl add salsa, sour cream and 1TBS of taco seasoning. MIX it, stir it! Give it some love! When it's done add it to the lettuce following with meat. Now mix the entire thing... Now thank me! As this is delicious. K Thanks.

Disclaimer: Taco Tuesday? How about taco salad every day! Tequila, taco salad and a telenovela... DONE

Game Time:

Instructions: Answer the question, then use the first letter of guessed word and put in the box below according to number. Remember *FIRST LETTER.*

1. What do you chew on?
2. Fill in the blank: Garden of ____ n.
3. Exotic animal with orange fur, black/white pattern.
4. Short for Richard.
5. When someone mugs you. You get _____ d.
6. One of the shows. MISS _____ e.
7. Popular game that features a plumber. Name the console
8. _____ Fried Chicken.

You can take this shot only if you complete the game. Otherwise - BYE

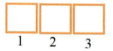
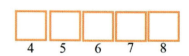

Urgent: If you are underage do not complete this step. Get a damn *Juice Box.*

Example for the not so smart specimens: For example if my guessed word is *England*. The letter I would use would be *E*

OH MY CABBAGE!

Red Cabbage Salad. UGH so good!

About the dish:

Red Cabbage! Very under rated veggie! This recipe is Sylvia's *(my sister)* special. Red cabbage salad is extremely popular in Poland. It is served inside of gyros, kebab and used a lot as a side dish! You will be surprised cabbage can taste so good. This dish is inspired on Silesia-Poland region. Where red cabbage dishes are quite popular. You should know that red cabbage is a good source of vitamin K and provides calcium, magnesium, and zinc, which can help build and maintain healthy bones. Red cabbage is high in fiber, making it easier to digest foods and keep your digestive system healthy. Voila! Again, David comes with information! Once again you learn something from this book! *Now let's go!*

Serving size: 4-5 humans!
Prep time: 10 Minutes. Give or take!
Cook Time: 5 minutes. It's only mixing!

Get This:

1 Red Cabbage: Get the size of your head... haha. Should be enough.

1 Large red onion - Large, once again SEAN not you.

4 TBS of Mayo - #DadJokeOfTheDay ... Put the bottle of mayo into the sink. Call your loved one over... Get a shot of tequila ready and point at the bottle and say... IT'S SINKO DE MAYO! Bottoms up! *(Not you Chris, gosh the Tequila!)*

2 teaspoons of vinegar - I was at the bar and this drunk guy asked this nice girl: *Am I hot? You dig it?* She replied: *If beauty was a drop of water, you'd be the Sahara Desert.*

Half of an apple - Tell me, as an outsider, what do you think of the human race?

Salt and pepper to taste.

Do This:

CUT the cabbage into skinny small pieces. Put gloves on, she can stain! Drop it into a large bowl. Cut the onion into little square pieces (Put titanic end scene on so your crying is justified), add vinegar follow with mayo.

MIX IT! Add apple, salt and pepper to taste. Mix, Mix, Mix! Let it sit for 15 minutes until flavors combine. That is, it. Easy Breezy Quick! Now time for a toast!

Disclaimer: Do not spill vinegar. The stench is terrible. Unless you're into sweaty feet! *

CRABSTER
(For the sea lovers) Super darn quick crab meat salad!

About the dish:

This is a super quick salad. This is my sister's recipe. It is quick, efficient and tasty. If you like lemon, this is your go to. This is the quickest recipe in the entire book. Surprisingly tastes good with tortilla chips! Important info: Crab is packed with protein, which is important for building and maintaining muscle. Crab also contains high levels of omega-3 fatty acids, vitamin B12, and selenium. These nutrients play vital roles in improving general health while helping prevent a variety of chronic conditions. Lemons contain a high amount of vitamin C, soluble fiber, and plant compounds that give them several health benefits. Lemons may aid weight loss and reduce your risk of heart disease, anemia, kidney stones, digestive issues, and cancer according to recent studies. This dish contains both! I might say it is super healthy. Once again David, you did not fail of making your chefs smarter! *Let's go.*

Pg.115

Serving Size: 1 - Just one. If you want more *(for the non-mathematical specimens just multiple the recipe by how many people you want to feed).*

Prep time: 5 minutes - Quick and easy!

Cook time: 1 minute - Voila! It is just mixing.

Get This.

1 Cup of cooked lump crab meat - My friend got upset at her hubby and said: *You've got your head so far up your ass you can chew your food twice.* He replied: *I heard that you went to the haunted house and they offered you a job.*

1/4 cup of corn - #DadJokeOfTheDay - Should you eat corn that has fallen off the stalk? Maize Well! Please do not cancel me!

1 radish shredded - Well then... You look radishing! – LAME-O!

3/4 cup of spinach — My little neighbor goes: *What is the difference between spinach and boogers?* Kids do not eat spinach. Eww… Nasty little fuc*ers.

1 Teaspoon arugula mix - #AnotherDadJokeOfTheDay - If you are a DAD and you are using this book. You are not arugula DAD! Please tell me you get the joke. No? Okay... well sh*t.

2 Tablespoons of lemon - My friend's kid goes: *You've got the perfect weapon against muggers. Your face.*

salt for taste *Optional:* Diced avocado.

Do This.

I WILL keep this short this time. Mix it all. Done!

Disclaimer: No, I did not get bored writing this. This is not why this recipe is so short and quick. Shut up. *

Polish Kopytka
(Sort of like gnocchi kind of better)

About the dish:

Polish kopytka *(pron. Coo-pit-ka)* is a traditional side dish! Specialty of both my grandma and mother. This recipe originated in Greater-Poland in the late 1600's. King John III Sobieski (yes there's Vodka that bears his name) brough potatoes to Poland in 1683 after the battle of Vienna. History: The Battle of Vienna took place at Kahlenberg Mountain near Vienna on 12 September 1683 after the imperial city had been besieged by the Ottoman Empire for two months. The battle was fought by the Holy Roman Empire led by the Habsburg Monarchy and the Polish–Lithuanian Commonwealth, both under the command of Polish King John III Sobieski, against the Ottomans and their vassal and tributary states. The Ottoman army numbered approximately 300,000 men… While Polish Hussars *(Winged soldiers – known as ANGELS do to their armor and its big feather wings in the back)* had 20,000 men. If not for winning this battle, whole Europe could have been lost to Ottoman Empire. Therefore, Polish are such bad asses! Anyways, thanks to this man potatoes came to Poland – and now we have this dish. Woah, this was a long history lesson! Again, you are becoming smarter! You are welcome!

Get This:

Serving: 4 human beings!
Prep Time: 10-15 minutes.
Cook Time: 15 minutes!

2 cups mashed potatoes cold - *(Great time to use the left-over potatoes!)* See you are utilizing! If you do not have leftovers. Just do basic type mash potatoes *(no powder cr*p)*. Let them get cold. Kind of like your relationship with your neighbor.

1 large egg - Large is not a word we would describe the hubby! You know it, I know it!

1 cup all-purpose flour - #DadJokeOfTheDay - What kind of flour is independent? Self-Rising flour... I know lame... I will get my coat. Bye.

*Disclaimer: This pairs well with a lot of different sauces, alcohol, alcohol and alcohol. *

Do This:

PLACE mashed potatoes in a mixing bowl. They should be cold, so this is a great way to use up leftover potatoes like I said above. Add egg and flour and mix until the dough comes together. Place dough onto a floured surface and divide into two parts. Roll one part of the dough into a long log (You wish it were your nick name Sean, it is not) and slice into 1.5 to 2" dumplings.

IN A large saucepan or pot, boil water and add 1 teaspoon of salt. Add 8 to 10 dumplings at a time to the boiling water and cook until they start to float at the top (kind of like my whale self in the pool). Remove and place on a plate. Repeat with remaining dumplings.

There is two ways of serving these suckers!

WAY NUMER 1!

In a skillet, heat up 1 tablespoon of oil and 1 tablespoon of butter. Add cooked dumplings – fry until golden brown. Remove onto a plate. Add 2 minced garlic cloves, 1 small yellow onion (chopped. Sauté until fragrant. Toss with dumplings and serve. Also, can be paired with gravy!

WAY NUMBER 2 (My favorite personally)

In a skillet, heat up 1 tablespoon of oil, toss the dumplings on hot oil until golden on both sides, add salt and pepper... GREAT for a side.

*Disclaimer: This pairs well with a lot of different sauces, alcohol, alcohol and alcohol. *

The David-Mash – Potatoes!

About the dish:

Well, well, well, potatoes are surely my favorite! Call me a *Potato-h*e*. Paired with onion, garlic, parsley & bacon... *Oink, oink* ... What can go wrong?! This was an accidental recipe by yours truly... I do not regret it – it is super yummy! This side dish goes with basically with any meat dish! It is not hard, quite easy. So, take a sip of some liquor or water and lets go!

Pg.119

Serving: IDK maybe 5.
Prep Time: 5 mins, unless you take your sweet time.
Cook Time: 15 mins usually.

Get This:

6 Large Gold potatoes - (Or any other not sweet potatoes - whatever you got laying around Cinderella....).

1/4 cup of milk - MAMA likes milk! Unless you are LACTOSE INTOLERANT... Make sure you find the nearest EXIT.

2 Tablespoons of sour cream - Unless you cannot stand it then don't add it why listen to me anyways it's not like I'm writing a cookbook or anything.

1/6 cup butter - My friend to her husband: *If I ever need a brain transplant, I'd choose yours because I'd want a brain that had never been used.* Ouch!

1 cup Parmesan cheese - He replied to her: *What are you going to do for a face when the baboon calls and wants his ass back?* Touche!

1/2 cup chopped fresh parsley - My grandpa got into a small fight with his neighbor and said: *If I wanted to listen to an asshole, I'd fart.*

1/2 cup cream cheese – My neighbor's son asked his grandfather how old is grandma? He replied: *Grandma is so old; she was a waitress at The Last Supper.* Ouch!

4 Cloves of garlic - For the people who live alone and do not date- add more garlic it's not like your breath matters tonight anyways ......

1 pinch salt and pepper to taste - #DadJokeOfTheDay - "What did the janitor say when he jumped out of the closet?" - "Supplies!"

1/2 cup of BACON – Fry it, crumble it after. Also, for the tired parents tell your kid the crushed bacon is *PEPPA PIG* jigsaw puzzle... VIDEO their reaction please!

AND for the last ingredient blast a song you enjoy take a damn shot of liquor *(unless you are underage... Wow now I would also be blamed for creating alcoholics)* do a 30 second dance, swirl 3 times and clap 2............ Please tell me you ignored this one and did not proceed... We are not summoning demons here just cooking.... I mean the shot part... Take it. Why limit yourself.

Do This:

BRING a pot of salted water to a boil. Peel then cut potatoes into smaller pieces – drop in the pot cook until tender but still *FIRM (yeah everything is firm until you pass 30... anyone needs TAPE?)* Around 10-15 mins.

AFTER potatoes are done, drain the water. If you are using a kitchen aid to mash our potatoes it is time to transfer them in the kitchen aid. If you are doing it by hand leave it in the pot.

ADD butter *(I hope you figured the measurements by now !!)* add parmesan cheese, parsley, cream cheese, garlic, salt, pepper, milk, sour cream, and finally BACON!! Use a potato masher to mash until smooth and serve. *(Unless you are a lazy fart like me and do not need extra gym day mashing the potatoes throw everything into your kitchen aid and let all mix automatically).*

FINALLY finish with another shot, preferably gargle it... You might wonder why. Well... in case you totally screw this recipe up, at least after gargling and burning your taste buds with shots you will not really taste the dish anyways. Win, win? After you finish, garnish with some additional parsley.

*DISCLAIMER: You are a potato! *

Let's play a game!

```
F M D O D U M B P H C U N T Y
V Q E T D A S S A S S H O L E
E T V Z W I D I O T F O B D R
T B I T W A T V A U U D U N D
R S L A U R T L I P G R F E Z
A H R C N R J S V I L N L N N
S I F O L O C F I D Y L C U D
H T F A I G J A U C E P Z E O
C F U Q K A P T N C L Q S D N
R A C D A N P Z N N N E S L K
I C K V B T I A R V O H H A E
N E E L L T C E D I C Y X O Y
G B R S E X S O I I Q U I T L
E Z O R K O L K C E K S L N M
Y Z Y R L X L Q K B M H R Q G
```

Instructions:

This is your moment to finally let go. Think about someone you do not like. Can be your boss, family member, ETC! First 5 words you find – Describes them. Have fun insulting them. Let loose!

Take a shot to let your brain loose!
Only if you are 21+ if not, get a juice box.

Pg.121

Garlic-zilla Fries!

Honestly bomb AF... If you do not know what AF stands for... Internet helps;)

About the dish:

Oh fries! *Who does not like them?* No, they were not invented in France... as the name suggests. Well, okay I mean it is a dispute between Belgium and France who invented these. See wow this book also brings world class knowledge. You're welcome. Now you are 10% smarter and 15% heavier and might need Botox after laughing or cringing at all this content. Anyways, these are great garlic - parsley fries! Once you try it - you will want more! Okay let us get fat and sassy! *LET'S GO!*

Serving: 6 perhaps... For me though - it is like 1 serving as I'm a Potato-hoe.

Prep Time: 15 minutes. Don't mess up.

Cook time: 15 minutes. You burned your finger.. Did ya?

Get This:

10 large russet potatoes peeled and rinsed - Honestly not going to lie, you can use any potatoes for this don't have to be russet. #DadJokeOfTheDay - *Why do potatoes make great detectives? Because they always keep their eyes peeled...*

2 quarts vegetable oil can sub canola oil – I seen these two kids arguing in the store - One shouts loud as heck! *Yo mama so tall, she tripped over a rock and hit her head on the moon.* Kid got them jokes!

Salt/Pepper - To taste... Will not work on you though.

1/2 cup of Fresh chopped parsley - My friend swears he is a bartender... Therefore, the other day I asked for a Manhattan. He is excited ready to nail this... The drink comes and I see a piece of parsley floating around. I'm like *what the f*ck is this, Sean?* He responds - *Central Park David!* Never asking him for a drink again.

1/2 cup minced garlic - Angry wife to her husband: *Your only purpose in life is to become an organ donor.* He replied: *I could eat a bowl of alphabet soup and poop out a smarter statement than whatever you just said.* She yelled: *I have seen people like you. But I had to pay admission.* He calmly ended with: *You look like a 'before' picture. The last time I saw a face like yours, I fed it a banana.*

Do This:

SLICE the potatoes into ½ inch thick sticks (look at any fashion show for reference). Using a French fry cutter makes this much easier. Time to invest in one!

TIP: If you want your fries to be extra crispy, soak the potato slices in cold water for a minimum of one hour. The longer, the better as this process removes the starch which makes for extra crispy fries. Then rinse them twice with cold water. Try to pat them dry with paper towel.

HEAT oil in a deep fryer, dutch oven, or simply a pot to 300 degrees F - or if you cannot tell the temperature use medium setting. You will need to fry in about six batches, begin with a quart of oil and add more as needed. TIP: Frying too many at once makes them less crispy. So do not mess up!

ADD potatoes to the oil and fry for about 6-7 minutes. The oil should bubble lightly, we are only heating the potatoes, we don't want them to crisp yet. Not just yet! After you finish doing this, place the cooked potatoes on a paper towel lined plate and fry the rest of the remaining batches.

INCREASE the heat to 400 degrees F or to high option on your stove and fry each batch a second time until they are crisp and golden-brown, about 5 minutes or so.

REMOVE them and place them on dry paper towels. Now get a bowl out, put them in the bowl. Add minced garlic and freshly chopped parsley - mix around. At the end add salt and pepper to taste. Take a damn shot! You deserve it.

*___Disclaimer:___ No potatoes were harmed in this recipe. You just probably cut your finger... Clumsy a*s. *

Game Time!

Do not cheat. Pick a color box. Make sure you think hard as it is a challenge. You must complete it, or your dog/cat dies *(If you do not have pets, you are not safe. If you won't complete this challenge your Engine Light will come on. If you do not have a car... My god... Your bike will get stolen... If you also do not have a bike... Then your phone will break)*. Yes, I just did that – now we are in binding agreement. Now pick a damn color box. Then flip the book around and read the text that was upside-down.

To find answers flip your book upside-down.

If you picked yellow box – For your challenge you must first take 1 shot of liquor. Then, you must come up to your spouse and tell him/her – Eat me baby – and shake your butt in their face. If you do not have a spouse sorry to say it is additional 2 shots to cure that loneliness. *If you picked green box* – Your boss told me to tell you that you are a fu*kface, text him/her that face... *If you picked orange box* – I just want to let you know you are basically Shrek, no challenge for you – life is hard enough with ILY². *If you picked red box* – You must do 25 jumping jacks, take 2 shots.

Vienna Sausage Rice Delight!

About the dish:

We had crab, had veggies, had potatoes now time for rice! This is a quick and easy rice recipe. You can add this to any meat side. This recipe is inspired by Latin America. Before you throw a chancleta saying DIOS MIOS! This is not an original Latin recipe… I know duh! I just said it is just inspired by it! Take a shot to calm down.

Get This:

Serving: About 4.

Prep Time: 10 minutes. Unless you are clumsy!

Cook Time: 15 minutes.

2 cups Water - *Why is the ocean always on time?* IT LIKES TO STAY CURRENT... Oh my! I give up on jokes today *slams doors* BAIIIII. Okay ... I am back.

1/4 cup Cooking Oil (any cooking oil will do)

1/4 cup Tomato Sauce - #DadJokeOfTheDay - *How do you fix a broken tomato?* TOMATO PASTE! ... I know I'm so lame!

1/2 Tbsp Sofrito Sauce - This one and the one right under can be found in Spanish isle at supermarket.

1 package Sazon con Culantro y Achiote <-- Don't ask me, I do not know how to pronounce it. No sé!

1 Package Chicken Bouillon Powder – Funny story.... My neighbor's son asked his grandfather *how old is grandma?* He replied: *Grandma is so old; she was a waitress at The Last Supper.* Ouch

2 cups Short Grain White Rice - Knock, Knock *Who is there*.... Rice .... *Rice Who?* *...Rice to meet you... Oh my! The jokes are going downhill from here. Ouch.

2 Cans Vienna Sausages, chopped - Fun fact... I love eating German sausages, but it always gives me the *WURST* farts... Wurst means sausage in German... Okay well this joke just died.

Do This:

IF you are one of the few that survived that travesty of jokes up there, WELCOME! Into a pot, add Cooking Oil (1/4 cup). Stir in Tomato Sauce (1/4 cup), Sofrito Sauce (2 teaspoon), Chicken Bouillon Powder (1 package), and Goya® Sazon con Culantro y Achiote (1 package). Stir, Stir, Stir AWAY! Add the Short Grain White Rice (2 cup), Vienna Sausages (2 can), Water (2 cup), and Salt (to taste). Stir. Listen, I get it you ask *Where are the funny parts* after that failed attempt on jokes up there, I am trying to keep this professional. I know sad.

BRING mixture to a boil, then reduce heat to medium. Cover and let cook for 15-20 minutes, or until water is evaporated. Stir halfway through. Serve with sides of choice and enjoy!

*Disclaimer: You might see a flying chancleta later! *

Fried Brussels Sprouts!

About the dish:

I will not lie when I was a child I did not like brussels sprouts at all! Until I stumbled upon fried brussels sprouts. I decided to create my own garlic onion spin of this dish. It is super delicious! Trust me! I used to dislike them! But now, I love it! This is a quick and super easy recipe. Little fact according to recent studies. Brussels sprouts are high in fiber, vitamins, minerals and antioxidants, making them a nutritious addition to your diet. They may also come with added health benefits, including the potential to reduce the risk of cancer, decrease inflammation and improve blood sugar control. This information was provided by internet research. *Anyways! Okay, lets get going!*

Get This:

Serving: 4-5 human beings.
Prep Time: 10 minutes, give or take.
Cook Time: 20 minutes.

Some oil for frying.

1 cup chopped red or yellow onions - #DadJokeOfTheDay - *"What does a sprinter eat before a race?" "Nothing, they fast!"*… I understand I am no comedian. Thanks!

3 garlic cloves minced – My neighbors' kid really have some jokes. The other day he yelled this to some other kid: *Yo mama so old, her birth certificate is in Roman numerals.* This kid always makes me laugh.

1 lb. brussles sprouts, tops removed, halved – I have seen people like you. But I had to pay admission.

Freshly grated Parmesan cheese, to your liking (I used about 1/2 cup or so) – My nephew asked my grandpa: *how old is grandma?* He replied: *her social security number is 1*…

Salt and Pepper to taste.

Do This:

IN A large skillet, heat 2 tbsp olive oil briefly over medium heat. Add chopped onions and sauté until they are soft and nicely caramelized (5 to 7 minutes). Add garlic and toss another 30 seconds. Remove onions and garlic to a side plate for now. You will need it later!

ADD some oil to the pan again. If needed raise heat to medium-high, till oil is shimmering but not smoking. Add brussels sprouts flat-side down first. Cook and do not stir or turn over until bottoms crisp up, turning a nice golden brown or even charred. Turn-over on the other side and cook another 4-6 minutes until crisp.

TOSS in the cooked onions, garlic and parmesan cheese. And add a generous sprinkle of salt and pepper to taste. If you have some at home, you can also add bacon.

FUN FACT: These are the most drawn numbers in lottery. Do whatever you want with this information. If you win 50% is mine.

22, 11, 9, 10, 19, 61, 53, 69, 64, 3, 21, 27, 62

If you don't win - well it is what it is.

*Disclaimer: You might get addicted to this dish! *

Take a shot! You deserve it!
If you are not 21+ get a juice box.

Welcome to My Sister

Sylwia Rzegocka – No there is no mistake in her name ''w'' is used and sounds like ''v'' in the Polish language. She is the mother of my lovely nephew Sebastian Falcon which you will also see in this book in this chapter. Sylwia, is a kind and loving person. Drives like she has an extra life! She always supports me and vice versa. Best thing about her? Well, maybe the fact that it is never boring when she enters your life! Fun to party with, fun to hang out with with! I would not have asked for a better sister! Therefore, I wanted to include her in this book. She will present you with her 3 recipes! She is a *sea lover* so all her picks are…. Well sea food! *Enjoy!*

This little cutie in the corner is my *nephew & godson Sebastian*. My mini me! Kind, loving and caring child. Despite being only 5 this year *(2021)* he's the sweetest little kiddo out there. You will see him on few of the pages in this book. Mine and his bond is unbreakable! Kid stole my heart since birth. Unlce loves you!

SCALLOPS LA LOCA

Don't worry you will not go crazy after.

About the dish:

Why this name? Well, it is my sister's recipe. She's Loca.. *(to the less informed people - Loca is a female term for crazy in Spanish language - but in a good way... at least in this instance).* Well, let me introduce you to my lovely sister. She is the one that drives like we got extra lives... Great mom and a good cook! This is a recipe for her scallops. She is crazy about seafood. Hence the name Scallops La Loca. That is all she could eat. Seriously! Its super tasty if you are into scallops! Give it a go!

Serving: 3 humans, one horse.
Prep Time: 10 minutes.
Cook Time: 20 minutes.

Get This:

For the Scallops:

10 Large Scallops - #DadJokeOfTheDay - Have you heard the story of a scallop? A scallop fell in love with a clam...and against everyone's advice they got married. Six short months later sure enough they filed for divorce and went their separate ways. Their damn problem was obvious to anyone who knew them, they were just two shellfish. *I am cancelling myself*

1 Lemon -Two wrongs don't make a right, take your parents as an example.

2 TBS of chives cut to tiny pieces - My grandma goes: *Grandpa is so old that he gets nostalgic when he sees the Neolithic cave paintings.* My grandpa: *Grandson, your grandmothers first car was a dinosaur.*

Salt and pepper to taste - #AnotherDadJokeOfTheDay: *"What does a lemon say when it answers the phone?" "Yellow!"* – Get it?

3 Tablespoons of ghee – Grandpa goes: *What did one ocean say to the other ocean?* ME: *I don't know what?* Grandpa: *Nothing, it just waved.*

FOR SIDE ASPARAGUS (Optional)

Fresh asparagus - Every supermarket has them in the fresh aisle usually held with a rubber band. Get one. Use one. Voila.

2 Garlic gloves - My neighbor kid is a clever one. He took me aside and said: *My mama so scary, the government moved Halloween to her birthday.* Kid got me laughing my as* off!

1 Cup of panko breadcrumbs - *Before I break down and rye, I want you to know that I loaf you.* --- My crappy attempt to be funny.

pepper & salt – for taste as usual.

Pg.131

Do This:

THIS is going to be quick!

IF scallops are frozen *(just like your face expression after all that Botox)*, thaw in cold water - won't work for your face, sorry. Remove the side muscle from the scallops if attached. Thoroughly pat dry with paper towels. If they are fresh skip this step.

GET your skillet out. Heat up the Ghee *(Oh my gheeee Carol)*. Add scallops, salt, pepper, lemon juice, chives. Cook for 6 minutes! Set aside. Serve with asparagus as a side!

****Disclaimer:*** Look at our cute family photos! Also, you are welcome for a wonderful dish!

TO MAKE QUICK ASPARAGUS

GET fresh asparagus, fry on medium for 5-6 minutes.

ADD salt, pepper to taste.

ONCE its softer, add 2 gloves of minced garlic, and about 1 cup of panko breadcrumbs. Serve as a side.

Scary Monsters
Crab Legs

About the dish:

You might ask: *Why scary monsters David?* Well, my nephew Sebastian calls crab legs… scary monsters! He loves them, I love them and so will you. This is served with lemon juice and cilantro but if you are a butter lover you can do butter as well. This recipe is my sisters special. She makes crab legs all the damn time! I mean crab meat has a lot of benefits such as: Promotes mental health. Crab meat is enriched with protein, zinc and omega 3 fatty acids which can improve cognition and concentration. It also helps in strengthening myelin, a lipid-rich fatty substance formed in the central nervous system and protects the nervous system, while also reducing plaque and inflammation in neural pathways. This knowledge is not according to me… But the everything-knowing internet! Okay, let us not waste more time. This is an extremely easy recipe! *Let's get going!*

Serving: 5 Humans! Maybe 6.
Prep Time: 5 minutes. If you are not clumsy!
Cook Time: 45 minutes. It is really not that long.

Get This:

4 lb. Crab Legs (not king crab) – #DadJokeOfTheDay - A guy walks into a seafood store carrying a crab, he asked the owner, *"Do you make crab cakes?"* And the owner said, *"Yes we do."* ...So the guy said, *"Good because it's his birthday."*

4 heaping TBS cup of garlic powder – My friend's kid goes: *What does garlic and my dad have in common?* ME: *What?* Him: *They both stink....*

4 TBS of Maggi Seasoning Sauce (it is in a bottle looks like soy sauce) – Oh my same kid from above said this to me as well... *My dad is so big, his belt size is an "equator."*....

4 heaping TBS adobo all seasoning spice – Well kid tried third time.... He said: *My dad so short, when he went to see Santa, he told him to get back to work....* Dad heard this time. Kid got grounded. I think he will be a comedian!

3 chicken bouillon cubes – My neighbor got upset at my other neighbor and shouted: *Some babies were dropped on their heads but you were clearly thrown at a wall.* The other guy did not wait long and responded: *Why don't you slip into something more comfortable... like a coma.*

1 TBS of red pepper flakes – My friend got upset at her husband. She yelled: *You are so fat that when you wear a yellow raincoat people shout out "taxi".* He responded: *Well, you're so fat that the most complicated origami has less folds than you.* They are still married if you wondered.

4 heaping TBS of old bay spice – #AnotherDadJokeOfTheDay - *Why was grandma in such a hurry while making pasta sauce for the dinner guests?* It was already 8pm and she was running out of thyme. Gee, David you are so lame! Ha-ha!

2 TBS black pepper – My grandmother got upset at my grandpa and shouted: *You're so old that you owe Moses a dollar.*

<u>FOR DIPPING SAUCE:</u>

½ fresh cut cilantro – I was at the store, and this lady walked up to the cashier and said: *You have an extremely kind face, the kind you throw bricks at.* I do not know what he did. But I would not want to be him.

6 lemons – *How old are you?* - Wait I shouldn't ask, you can't count that high.

U got it

Do This:

THIS will be quick and simple. Get a small bowl out. Squeeze all the lemons in the bowl, add in chopped cilantro. Mix. Keep the squeeze halves.

GET a large deep pot out. Fill it with water all the way leaving 2.5'' on the top. Add all the ingredients in. Mix do not take shells off the crab. Place legs as you bought it, whole in the pot. Add squeezed lemon halves into the pot. Cook on medium/low for about 45 minutes. If water over boils reduce the heat.

ONCE crabs are done, serve! Enjoy!

*__Disclaimer:__ You might get addicted to this dish. I know I did. *

Was this easy?

👍 YES ☐   👎 NO ☐

GAME: Pick a cup. Then flip the book around to reveal answer.

NUMBER 1: Take an embarrassing selfie and post it as your profile picture. Also, take a shot.
NUMBER 2: Never have I ever: Never have I ever hooked up with someone I met online. Never Have I Ever had a crush on my friend's partner. Never Have I Ever stalked someone on Instagram. Never Have I Ever regretted dating someone. - Amount of answers = amount of shots.
NUMBER 3: Flip a cup! Set one plastic cup face down on the edge of a table or counter. Try to flip it so it stands up. You have 3 tries. If you fail you need to chug 2 shots. If you will not participate - your ENGINE light will come on.

Pg. 135

The Grand Baked Oysters!

About the dish:

I told you my sister is addicted to seafood. Presenting to you awesome baked oysters. **Fun Fact:** Oysters have a lot of health benefits. According to research oysters are a Rich Source of Omega-3 Fatty Acids. An Excellent Source of Protein. Oysters Are Extremely Rich in Zinc. Zinc is an important mineral that has many functions in the human body. ... Rare Food Source of Vitamin D. Vitamin D functions as a hormone rather than a traditional vitamin, and it plays a crucial role in keeping the human body. See, they are not only delicious but also healthy! I hope you enjoy this recipe like I have! *Let's get going!* Take a deep shoot of liquor…. Or water!

Servings: 4 servings, about 12 oysters.
Prep Time: 20 minutes.
Cook Time: 12 minutes.

Get This:

1 dozen fresh oysters, in the shell - Someone insulted my big friend. She straight up replied: *I am not fat, I'm hot and everyone knows that things expand when they are hot, it's science.* Girl killed it.

2 cups rock salt or uncooked rice, for lining the pan - My neighbor's kid is a real comedian. This lady yelled at him for running at the pool. He yelled back: *I thought whales do not talk! Get back into the water Shamu.* I literally choked on my drink.

1 teaspoon finely grated lemon zest - If you do not know how to zest a lemon kindly find out online.

1 stick (8 tablespoons) salted butter, softened, divided - #DadJokeOfTheDay: I would tell you a butter joke, however I am afraid you will SPREAD it! Ha-ha get it. No? Damn.

3/4 cup panko breadcrumbs - Funny story. Once at school our teacher wanted to educate us students about self-esteem, so she asked anyone who thought they were stupid to stand up. My friend stood up and the teacher was really surprised. She did not anticipate that anyone would stand up, so she asks him, *"Why did you stand up?"* He answers, *"I didn't want to leave you standing up by yourself."* He got detention next day.

2 tablespoons finely chopped chives - Chop, chop!

1 tablespoon lemon juice - *What does lemon and you have in common?* You both can be sour bit*hes.

Sweet paprika, optional - You know you are big when a doctor says, *"I need your weight not your phone number."*

Chopped fresh parsley, garnish - Always fresh! Unlike your style... Who said that!

2 to 3 wedges lemon, for serving - My friend to her husband: *You must have been born on a highway because that's where most accidents happen.* He replied: *Your family tree must be a cactus because everybody on it is a prick - including you.*

Pg.137

Do This:

PREHEAT the oven to 430 F. Add a layer of rock salt to a baking pan so you can keep our oyster shells from wobbling. Scrub these lovely oyster shells with a stiff brush. Carefully shuck the oysters over a bowl to catch any liquids that might or might not spill out. Run the knife along the bottom of the inside of the shell to loosen the oyster. If some of the oyster liquor does spill out, return it to the bottom shell. Discard the top shells and arrange the oysters with their liquid in the prepared baking pan.

NEXT, in a skillet over medium heat, melt about 4 tbs of butter. Then add panko crumbs and cook, stirring, until the crumbs are lightly browned. Set aside.

NOW, in a bowl, combine the remaining softened butter with: lemon juice, chives and the lemon zest. Then, top each oyster with a scant teaspoon of the butter-and-chives mixture and then sprinkle each one with our buttered panko crumbs. If you decided to use paprika sprinkle some on top.

NOW, comes the baking. Bake these lovely oysters in the preheated oven for about 8 to 10 minutes, or until the oysters are cooked through and the topping is golden brown. Sprinkle with fresh chopped parsley. Then, serve with lemon wedges. The end. You had done it!

__Disclosure:__ Make sure you get fresh oysters as you might end up in the toilet. Stock up on toilet paper in case. *

Sebastian and his mommy are proud of you!

Board Of Positivity!

This is where you will find some good alcoholic and non alcoholic beverages that can ease your cooking time or maybe even your day! Sincerley: *David Cole*

The Bikini Martini:

You will need: 1 fluid ounce coconut rum, ¾ fluid ounce vodka, 1 fluid ounce pineapple juice1, dash grenadine syrup.

How to make it: Combine rum, vodka and pineapple juice in a drink shaker. Shake firmly until frothy. Pour in a martini glass, add a touch of grenadine in the middle. Garnish with an orange wheel.

Rumsky Cocktail

You will need: 6 ozs of dark or light rum, 3 tbs lime juice, 2 tsp sugar, 1 and 1/2 cups crushed ice

How to make it: Place all ingredients into a blender. Blend for 20 seconds.

Strawberry Blueberry Lemonade

1 and half cup of lemonade, half cup of ginger ale, 2tbs mashed blueberries, 2tbs mashed strawberries, mint, 2 slices of lemon. MIX it all

Kiwi Lemonade!

1 and half cup of lemonade, half cup fresh mashed kiwi, 3 slices of lemon. Mix it all with ice. VOILA!

Pg. 139

BBQ Ribsies
It's just ribs.

About the dish:

Excellent ribs, both moist and tender. Great for that summer cookout. Yes, it takes some prep time and dedication. However, we both know good things come with time. What is better than a cold brew with a nice BBQ rib with great group of friends or family or even by yourself, why not! Make sure you clean your backyard; it looks like total sh*t! *Let's get going!*

Pg.141

Servings: About 7-ish
Prep time: 1 hour and 35 minutes! – *It is a process!*
Cook: 2 hours and 30 minutes ... Perhaps. – *Do not give up, it is worth it!*

Get This:

2 racks baby back ribs -... My aunts used to come up to me at weddings, poking me in the ribs and cackling, telling me, *"You're next."* They stopped after I started doing the same thing to them at funerals. *Bye Linda.*

2 cups barbecue sauce - Well you can make many choices here. I usually get a spicy BBQ sauce. But any sauce will work.

1/4 cup brown sugar - I do not have a joke for this one. Make your own.

1 cup low-sodium chicken broth - #DadJokeOfTheDay - *Why did the chicken cross the road?* -- To get to the idiot's house - Knock Knock. *Who's there?* The chicken.

2 tablespoons chili powder – Wife: *The janitor said he took out the trash last night, he must forgot a piece, what are you still doing here?* Husband: *If I had a dollar for every time you said something smart, I'd be broke. Are your parents siblings?*

1/2 teaspoon garlic powder – Next pandemic... Garlic The most effective social distancing enforcer. *Too soon?*

1/2 teaspoon cayenne pepper - another #DadJokeOfTheDay - A French man calls the room service and asks for some *"pepper"*. *"Well ... would you like some white pepper or black pepper?"* asks the receptionist. ---*"Toilet pepper."* - Replies the French.

1/2 teaspoon onion powder - I leave this one to you. Make a joke. Or just look in the mirror.

1 teaspoon dried oregano - Dried.... Just like my friend's grandma Edith. Opps. She's 105..

2 tablespoons apple cider vinegar - My friend Dennis used to call his wife "VINEGAR" why? Because according to him she was bitter as hell.

Kosher salt and freshly ground black pepper – To taste!

Do This:

MIX the brown sugar, 1 teaspoon black pepper, chili powder, 1 tablespoon salt, oregano, cayenne, onion powder and garlic powder in a small bowl, rub the mixture on both sides of the ribs, rub, rub baby! Cover and refrigerate for 1 hour or more if you can. Just do it. Stop complaining about time. Good things take time.

PREHEAT the oven to 255 degrees F. In a baking pan, mix broth and vinegar. Add the ribs to the pan. Cover with foil and tightly seal (cannot say the same thing about you. Definitely not tightly sealed anymore. Someone dropped a diaper?). Bake 2- 2,5 hours. Remove the ribs from the baking pan, place them on a plate. POUR the liquid from the pan into a saucepan and bring to a boil. Lower the heat to a simmer and cook until reduced by half. Add the barbecue sauce of your choice.

NOW for the goodie! Tastes better if you have a wood pallet for the grill you can lay the ribs on top. If not, it is okay. Proceed without it. Who cares!

PREHEAT an outdoor grill to medium/high. Grill ribs about 5 minutes on each side, until browned and slightly charred. Cut the ribs between the bones and toss them in a large bowl with the sauce. Serve hot (you used to be hot what happened? Marriage? I get it). Pairs well with mash potatoes! Find it in the SIDES chapter of this grand book.

I will save you some time! And drop additional recipe for:

Quick home-made bacon mash potatoes 4 large potatoes, ½ cup of cream cheese, 4 tablespoons of milk, 2 tablespoons of butter, ½ cup of finely chopped parsley, 6 slices of bacon fried and crushed. Directions: Peel 4 potatoes, cut them into small pieces, boil in the water for about 10-15 minutes (depends on the size of the potato cut) once boiled, mash the potatoes add cream cheese, milk, butter, parsley and crushed bacon. Season to taste with pepper and salt. If you want more creamy potatoes keep adding more milk.

Disclaimer: I ran out of jokes today; it is super late. I need someone to smack me the hell out of it. Hello? Sit down I am sure most of you would smack me with this book ha-ha-ha*

Pick one:

Chug one shot of vodka.   Chug one shot of tequila.   Under 21 Drink a juicebox.

Pg.143

Polish Krokiety & Naleśniki 2 in 1
Stuffed crepes

About the dish:

<u>Polish Naleśniki</u> *(nah-lesh-NEE-kee)*Don't giggle you ass** are crepe-like pancakes that can be made thin, as in this recipe, or as a thick one. They can be enjoyed with either sweet or savory fillings. Fillings can be as simple as your favorite jam, preserves, or fresh fruit such as berries. Spread them with some Nutella and add banana slices. I grew up on these. I turned out great, at least I think so... shut up...

<u>Polish Krokiety</u>: *(pron. Cro-khe-ti)* Polish Croquettes are thin, large pancakes filled either with meat or cabbage and mushrooms. The pancakes are coated with breadcrumbs and fried. This recipe has meat filling.

Servings: 12 servings (Or if you're a damn whale like me, probably less)

Prep: 35 mins unless you are complicated. Then may the faith be with you.

Cook: 20 mins - might be more if you burn things up.

Get This:

1/2 cup all-purpose flour - Okay, Sniffany stop with that straw!

1/2 cup milk - #DadJokeOfTheDay ... Milk bottles are hanging in the supermarket fridge, *hey Lauren* - one milk bottle says to the other - * look it is the new type of milk being added to the store today. *New Bottle Comes In* SOY MILK! .. Other milk bottles... *OH HE MUST BE FOREGIN! *.. The End.

1/4 cup water, lukewarm - Lukewarm... just like your sex life. I wrote it, you said it!

2 large beaten eggs - PASS! Says your husband. Ouch.

2 tablespoons unsalted butter melted - I would tell you a butter joke.... BUT you might just spread it... I know I am lame, cannot help it! Damnit!

1/2 teaspoon fine salt - Fine. That used to be you. What happened?

1 tablespoon unsalted butter, for frying - Don't burn your hands! ER is quite expensive in the States. Do you even have insurance?

FOR THE FILLING: If you choose to do krokiety instead.

1lb of ground meat – Any type of meat. I used turkey, as it tasted the best.

2 onions chopped – Anyone who thinks onions are the only vegetable that makes you cry. Has clearly never been hit in the face with a turnip. Ouch!

4 cloves of garlic – #AnotherDadJokeOfTheDay - *What does garlic do when it gets hot?* It takes its cloves off.

1 cup of chopped parsley - Fresh parsley!

4 cups of breadcrumbs - I usually get cheese flavored ones. But you can pick plain ones. *Like your EX.*

3 Large Eggs – Wife: *If I tell you I'm thinking about you, don't get too excited, because I'm also thinking about nachos.* Husband: *You have the right to remain silent because whatever you say will probably be stupid anyway.*

1 ½ Cup of shredded cheese – Preferably mozzarella!

Pg.145

Do This:

Filling: If making krokiety. Skip this if you are doing nalesniki and go to next page.

TAKE out a large bowl. Drop meat in it. Mix meat with 1 large egg, 2 cups of breadcrumbs, shredded cheese, parsley, onions, garlic add 1tbs of salt and pepper. Take out a pan, heat up some oil. Fry mixture on medium until done. Usually, 7-10 minutes or until it is done.

How to make krokiety:

IN a blender or food processor, combine the flour, milk, water, eggs, butter, and salt and then process until smooth. (If you do not own a damn blender... then just get a whisk and do a manual hard labor like it is 1920!) Transfer the batter to a bowl. Cover the bowl with plastic wrap and let it rest for 30 minutes so the liquid can be absorbed by the flour. Seriously, let it sit do not speed this up. Will not work in your favor!

HEAT a crepe pan or small skillet over medium heat and lightly coat with butter. Using a 2-ounce ladle, spoon one portion of the batter into the pan. (Don't F it up!) Immediately rotate the pan and swirl the batter until it covers the entire bottom. Cook until the crepe is lightly brown or spotted brown on the underside. Flip and cook the second side until it is light brown.-Remove the crepe to waxed paper (It is not time for a Brazilian wax Linda sit your ass down please) or parchment paper and repeat with the remaining batter. You may need to recoat the pan with butter as you cook the crepes.

PLACE about 2 heaped tablespoons of filling on each crepe. Fold it like you would fold a burrito: fold sides into the middle and then roll up the bottom tightly to the top. Some people spread the filling all over the crepe, leaving some border, and then fold them up. It is important to fold them tightly – they will be easier to fry.:

IN a bowl beat remaining eggs, bread the krokiety – dip them in beaten eggs then roll them in breadcrumbs until coated on all sides.

HEAT clarified butter or vegetable frying oil in a pan over medium heat. Cook the krokiety until golden brown on all sides. Transfer to a plate. Serve. You can dip it in hot nacho cheese.

How to make naleśniki:

YOU can make this dish in other way instead of krokiety, you can make them into naleśniki. Do everything needed to make a base. Which is same as krokiety. Spread 2 heaping tablespoons of savory filling or sweet filling on each naleśniki *(nutella, any jam, fresh fruits, etc.)*. Roll it into a roll. Do not fry serve rolled sprinkled with powdered sugar.

__Disclaimer:__ Take a hefty shot before making this. It will help you relax. JK I mean who knows.! You might need it.*

Let's play a game!

Instructions:

This is your moment to finally let go. Think about someone you do not like. Can be your boss, family member, ETC! First 5 words you find – Describes them. Have fun insulting them. Let loose!

```
F M D O D U M B P H C U N T Y
V Q E T D A S S A S S H O L E
E T V Z W I D I O T F O B D R
T B I T W A T V A U U D U N D
R S L A U R T L I P G R F E Z
A H R C N R J S V I L N L N N
S I F O L O C F I D Y L C U D
H T F A I G J A U C E P Z E O
C F U Q K A P T N C L Q S D N
R A C D A N P Z N N N E S L K
I C K V B T I A R V O H H A E
N E E L L T C E D I C Y X O Y
G B R S E X S O I I Q U I T L
E Z O R K O L K C E K S L N M
Y Z Y R L X L Q K B M H R Q G
```

Take a shot to let your brain loose!
Only if you are 21+ if not, get a juice box.

Pg.147

The Buttermilk Crispy Chick'n-Zilla Sandwich

About the dish:

Summer? Is that you? This buttermilk chicken sandwich will rock your world. Paired with my secret sauce it is to die for! It is easy to make, it does not take super long neither! This is inspired by Florida and the wonderful sun. If you are not from there… Well, close your eyes and imagine you are. If your house smells, I mean you can always be at a Floridian swap! You ogre. If you are not skilled in cooking, this should not be too much of an issue for you. I have faith in you. I mean nothing a solid shot cannot fix!
Okay, let us get going!

Serving: 6 humans. No cats!
Prep Time: 10 min.
Cook Time: 10 minutes.

Get This:

3 chicken breasts, boneless skinless – I remember the day my grandma got upset at my grandpa she said: You're not the dumbest person on the planet, but you sure better hope he doesn't die.

6 burger buns – Sesame seeds! Or you more of a plain person?

More ingredients on next page:

Lettuce, tomato, pickles, sliced cheese, red sliced onion!

Buttermilk marinade for crispy chicken-

1 cup buttermilk - Funny story…. I have none!

1 tsp salt - My friend asked me… *What does my wife and salt have in common?* I had no idea… He said they are both salty. Moments after a flip flop flew into his face.

¼ tsp ground black pepper - I asked my friend's kid *how old is his grandma?* He replied: *So old that she owes Moses a dollar.* I hope kid becomes a comedian.

Chick'n Breading-

1 cup all-purpose flour measured then sifted - I have no joke this time.

1 tsp ground paprika - My friend goes to his wife: Your family tree must be a cactus because everybody on it is a prick. Damn.

½ tsp garlic powder - Continuing the joke above. His wife replied: If I had a face like yours, I would sue my parents…. They are still married!

½ tsp onion powder - Since we are talking about my friend's marriage. They tend to fight a lot. Their fights are like TV roasts! Once my friend said: *You are so fake, Barbie is jealous…* She did not wait with a comeback and slammed him with: *When I see your face there is not one thing that I would change, apart from the direction that I was walking in.*

½ tsp ground black pepper - Make your own joke. Or look in the mirror.

1/4 cup cornstarch - Wait, my friend's marriage is so good I can tell you another story. Once his wife got mad and told him: *I would slap you, but that would be animal abuse.* He replied: *Some babies were dropped on their heads, but you were clearly thrown at a wall.* She did not hesitate to reply and said: *Why don't you slip into something more comfortable, like a coma….* They had been married for 10 years. How? I do not know.

1 tsp salt - This was supposed to be a joke. You showed up filling that spot.

Pg. 149

Sandwich Sauce:

1 cup of mayo – #DadJokeOfTheDay - What do you call a laughing jar of mayonnaise? Lmayo

1cup of BBQ sauce of choice - Any would do. I usually choose the average basic BBQ sauce.

½ cup of mustard of choice – Any mustard. I used spicy one. It was bomb.

½ cup of pickle juice – This is important. This is what makes this sauce… The banger!

2TBS of garlic powder – Once my mom told me garlic makes everything better… So, I sprinkled it at my parents' marriage certificate…. You have guessed it did not work instead – they divorced.

Do This:

Marinade:

CUT the chicken breast half giving you 6 chicken cutlets. Beat chicken with a meat mallet so it is even in thickness. Abusive much? Get that anger out. In a medium bowl, combine our buttermilk, salt and pepper. Place chicken in the buttermilk. Allow to marinate 35 minutes or overnight. If you want better flavor prior to placing chicken in the marinade, take a fork and stab it both sides this way buttermilk enters inside. *Oh my, this could be a good joke* But I will leave it alone. Next, mix all the ingredients for the breading. Take our lovely chicken from the buttermilk marinade and cover both sides of chicken with breading.

How to make sauce:

MIX all the sandwich sauce ingredients in a bowl. That is it! Voila!

How to Fry!

IN a large pot, add enough oil to completely cover chicken breast when submerged. Heat until oil is about 350°F. Once oil is hot, add the chicken and fry until golden and crispy, about 3-4 minutes per side. Next, transfer chicken to a place lined with a paper towel. To take out excessive oil. Once the chicken is done. Get buns out, and place lettuce, add some sauce, chicken, add more sauce, other toppings finish with another drop of sauce.

*_Disclaimer:_ The chicken can be frozen. If you do not wish to make 6 sandwiches fry only the ones you want to make. The rest you can freeze with marinade up to a month. *

1 PICK ONE **2**

I deserve a shot. I nailed this recipe. I screwed up.

David's Home-Made Margherita Pizza

About the dish:

Who does not love pizza? Pizza has a long history. Flatbreads with toppings were consumed by the ancient Egyptians, Romans and Greeks. *(The latter ate a version with herbs and oil, like today's focaccia.)* But the modern birthplace of pizza is southwestern Italy's Campania region, home to the city of Naples. This one is a margherita pizza, however you can add extra toppings as you wish! This recipe is not complicated so if you cannot cook for shizzle then this recipe is for you. Get going!

Pg.151

Serving: Two damn pizzas!
Prep Time: 15 minutes only! However rising time: 1 HR.
Cook Time: 10 minutes.

Get This:

DOUGH INGREDIENTS (MAKES 2 PIZZAS):

2 cups artisan bread flour - My friend has a remarkably interesting marriage. The other day he goes to his wife: *I am trying to see things from your point of view, but I can't get my head that far up my ass.* She did not wait long enough to respond and said: *Some babies were dropped on their heads, but you were clearly thrown at a wall.* Ouch. I don't need to watch tv. Just them.

3/4 cups warm water - Make sure its warm as its important!

1 teaspoon active dry yeast - #DadJokeOfTheDay: I replaced my dad's shaving cream with mayonnaise...He shouted, "what the Hellman!"

1.5 teaspoons sea salt - My friends' kid is a comedian! He goes to my friend: *Roses are red violets are blue, God made me pretty, what happened to you?*... Nothing to add!

TOPPING INGREDIENTS (FOR 2 PIZZAS):

olive oil + sea salt to brush over crust

8 ounces fresh mozzarella cheese, cut into 1/2-inch pieces (not packed in water is best) – My friend is trying to be a stand-up comedian. He tried one joke with me and said: *Why were mozzarella and feta holding hands? They look gouda together....* I said... Well Chuck you can already stand-up but you short on comedy!

1 ½ cup pizza or tomato sauce - #Another DadJokeOfTheDay: Why are tomatoes the slowest vegetable? Because they cannot ketchup.

4 tablespoons finely grated Parmigiano-Reggiano cheese,, plus more for serving – Never enough of cheese!

2 tomatoes sliced – Grandpa goes: *Why is the WIFI name Gump, and what is the password...?* Me: *The password is 1Forrest1.*

fresh basil, dried oregano, ground black pepper and red pepper flakes, to taste

Do This:

Pizza Dough:

COMBINE warm water and yeast in a large bowl. Add the flour and salt and stir with a wooden spoon until a dryish, shaggy-type dough forms. Transfer dough to a well-floured surface and knead until smooth and tacky, about 3-5 minutes. Work it! If dough is overly sticky, dust with more flour. Put the dough in a greased bowl and cover with a kitchen towel (or plastic wrap). Let it rise for 1 to 2 hours or until the dough has doubled in size. Divide dough into 2 separate balls. Balls!

How To Bake Our Pizza:

PREHEAT the oven to about 490-500°F. Roll and form into a circular disk. Then fold over edges to create a crust. You can get circular pizza pans at most stores. Makes the process easier.

How To Top Our Pizza:

DRIZZLE or brush the dough lightly with olive oil (about 1 teaspoon) and sprinkle on some sea salt. If you want your crust to have flavor sprinkle some garlic powder on top. Now spread sauce evenly and thinly over crust. Sprinkle the Parmigiano-Reggiano cheese over the pizza sauce. Next, add fresh mozzarella evenly over the pizza and top with sliced tomato. Gently slide the pizza onto a heated baking stone or baking sheet that is lined with parchment. If you have circular pizza pans just slide them in. Bake for 8 to 9 minutes, or until the crust is golden and the cheese is bubbling and caramelized. Remove the pizza from the oven and fresh basil, oregano, and red pepper flakes, if desired. Slice and serve immediately.

TIP FOR CRISPY CHICKEN PIZZA:

GET popcorn chicken from a grocery store. Cut it into small sizes sprinkle on top of the pizza. Instead of sliced mozzarella get shredded mozzarella instead and add extra Parmigiano-Reggiano on top. Then bake according to time mentioned above.

You deserve it:

*Disclosure: This can become your HIT dish! Wash your hands before making this. *

Fill it with whatever you want. Unless you are 21& under-then... Bye

Pg.153

Great Mongolian Beef

About the dish:

Mongolian beef! Is truly an art. This is a quick, easy and ridiculously delicious dish inspired by Mongolia. Little history: Mongolia, a nation bordered by China and Russia, is known for vast, rugged expanses and nomadic culture. Yes, Genghis Khan was from there. *What is Mongolian beef?* Mongolian beef is made from thin slices of meat, preferably flank steak, steamed in a brown soy sauce, mixed with vegetables, and eaten with either noodles or rice. In this recipe we will use NY strip steak. Okay, less talking more cooking! Take a heavy shot of vodka!

Serving: about 4 to 5!
Prep Time: 10 minutes.
Cook Time: about 15 minutes.

Get This:

Salt and pepper to taste.

2 New York Strip Steaks thinly sliced (about 1 1/2 pounds) - New York is the city that never sleeps, which is why it looks like hell in the morning.

⅓ cup low sodium soy sauce - #DadJokeOfTheDay: I Wonder if Soy sauce, is a regular sauce introducing itself in Spanish? Any thoughts? Si? No?

⅓ cup water - Funny story from my friend:

HIM: "Hey, I bet you're still a virgin."
HIS FRIEND: "Yeah, I was a virgin until last night."
HIM: "As if."
HIS FRIEND: "Yeah, just ask your sister."
HIM: "I don't have a sister."
HIS FRIEND: "You will in about nine months."

½ cup dark brown sugar - Hopefully, this will sweeten you up a bit you sour patch.

3 tablespoons cornstarch - #AnotherDadJokeOfTheDay: Light travels faster than sound. Therefore, some people appear bright until you hear them speak. AKA you.

3 green onions sliced into 1-inch pieces - My friend thinks he is smart. He told me an onion is the only food that makes you cry, so I threw a coconut at his face. He changed his mind.

2 teaspoon toasted sesame seeds optional - Once my friends kid got detention. According to him this is what happened. HIS OLDER TEACHER: "If I say, 'I am beautiful,' which tense is that?" HE REPLIED: "It is obviously past."... Poor kid was just honest.

3 tablespoons vegetable oil, divided - Divided... Like your parents after a divorce.

4 cloves garlic, minced - R.I.P Garlic... You will be minced! Get it?

1 tablespoon minced ginger - Please do not mince any Irish people.

steamed rice for serving - Steamed... Is your body after 2 steps up the stairs.

Pg.155

Do This:

SEASON your lovely, sliced steak with salt and pepper. How much? Well, to your damn liking. Toss steak in cornstarch coat it fully and evenly. Set aside. Now, place a large skillet over medium-high heat and add 2 tbs of oil. Then, add ginger, minced garlic and sauté for 2 minutes. Next, add soy sauce, sugar and water - bring to a boil until sugar dissolves, about 2-3 minutes.

ONCE you do the above, pour sauce into a liquid measuring cup - set aside. Now, place your skillet back over-heat and add remaining oil. Time to add steak and sear until evenly browned on both sides, about 2 to 3 minutes per side. Pour sauce back into skillet and toss together with meat. Allow sauce to thicken, about another 2 to 3 minutes.

NOW, toss in green onion and continue to cook for 1 more minute until sauce is thick enough to coat the back of your wooden spoon. Pour your lovely and delicious Mongolian beef over steamed rice and serve immediately.

*_Disclaimer:_ Do not mess this up. Also, do not burn yourself. K thanks, bye. *

T	B	R	E	H	H	T	A	S	T	V	O	T	A
C	A	U	B	N	T	N	O	T	H	I	N	G	H
N	B	U	R	E	I	R	V	A	Q	E	H	T	U
P	W	B	L	B	T	E	Q	U	I	L	A	O	C
V	U	T	K	I	O	G	T	T	N	B	E	E	R
O	Q	H	R	U	N	N	U	S	I	K	V	E	H
D	K	O	C	O	U	E	W	L	R	A	H	U	U
K	Q	C	T	T	I	D	N	H	Y	C	O	H	T
A	O	B	C	I	E	G	P	E	C	H	T	H	E
R	E	A	B	H	D	K	K	E	N	Y	S	A	I
U	H	E	W	E	E	S	D	B	I	E	A	T	Q
W	A	T	E	R	I	L	Y	K	G	Q	U	I	E
E	A	H	P	H	I	U	R	U	U	O	C	K	E
K	I	N	W	K	E	T	W	A	T	V	E	A	T

WHISKEY
GIN
BEER
KETCHUP
TEQUILA
WATER
VODKA
NOTHING
HOT SAUCE

Let's Play A Game!

You are obligated to play this game. On the side you have few words you can find. You only need one. Whatever you find you must take a whole *SHOT* – of whatever you found first. No EXEPTIONS! Sadly, if you are under 21 your only options are: water, hot sauce, nothing and ketchup…. I know 21 will eventually come!

Paprika Porkie In Creamy Sauce

About the dish:

Well, hello chefs! I thought I will introduce one more pork dish before I wrap this chapter up. This is a pork in creamy sauce! It is yummy! It is quick! For our specimens that cannot cook for sh*t this dish can be a life saver as it is not complicated! You are welcomed! Dish is inspired by summer! *I mean don't we all love summer?* I know I do. Okay, well take a deep shot of preferred liquor, water or whatever the hell you drink these days and let's get going!

Get This:

Servings: 4 humans, one dog.
Prep Time: 5 minutes.
Cook Time: about 15 minutes.

1 pork tenderloin (1 pound), preferably cut into 1" cubes – My friends have an interesting marriage. On one occasion my friend Catherine goes to her husband: *You're so fat, the photo I took of you last Christmas is still printing.* Oh no, do not worry he did not wait long with responding and said: *You are so fat that when you wear a yellow raincoat people shout out "taxi".* Secret to long marriage? Roast each other, I guess! It works for them.

1/4 teaspoon pepper - #DadJokeOfTheDay - I got hit in the head with a can of Dr. Pepper today. Luckily, I am not hurt, it was a soft drink. Oh, gee my jokes get lamer by day!

Minced fresh parsley – R.I.P Parsley, you will be minced! – Get it? No?

1 tablespoon butter - #AnotherDadJokeOfTheDay- I have a great butter joke I could tell you. However, I am afraid you will spread it!

3/4 cup heavy whipping cream - My neighbor kid goes to me the other day. ''Heavy, that is what the weight scale says when you stand on it''. Listen little sh*it I am only 145lb.!

Hot cooked egg noodles or rice - I was once in Paris. I tried to order some eggs, the waiter goes: How many French eggs do you need? Me trying to sound international I replied ''One egg is un oeuf.'' She did not seem like she appreciated it. Her expression looked like she choked on a sour patch.

1 teaspoon all-purpose flour - All purpose. Like you. I didn't say it... Your spouse did.

4 teaspoons paprika - My friend's name is PEPE and his last name is RICCA. Really no joke. I think his parents liked cooking.

3/4 teaspoon salt - Oh, my dear friends' marriage. Why do I mention it a lot...? Well because it is funny as heck! My friend Chuck goes to his wife and says: I am not saying that you are stupid, just that you are constantly unlucky when you try thinking. Well to the true roaster that Catherine is she didn't wait long and responded: You are so stupid that if we were invaded by zombies, you would be completely safe because zombies eat brains – and you my love got none!

Do This:

TOSS our lovely porkie with flour and seasonings. Get a large skillet, heat butter over medium heat; saute porkie until lightly browned, 4-6 minutes.

NOW please add cream; bring to a boil, stirring to loosen browned bits from pan. Cook, uncovered, until cream is slightly thickened, about maybe 5-7 minutes.

FINALLY: Serve with noodles. Sprinkle with minced parsley.

*_Disclaimer:_ This is a quick recipe! I told you so. However, you never listen! *

Game time!

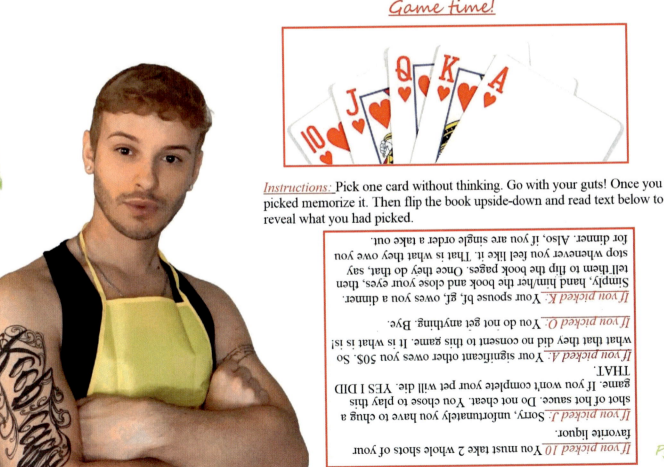

Instructions: Pick one card without thinking. Go with your guts! Once you picked memorize it. Then flip the book upside-down and read text below to reveal what you had picked.

If you picked K: Your spouse bf, gf, owes you a dinner. Simply, hand him/her the book and close your eyes, then tell them to flip the book pages. Once they do that, say stop whenever you feel like it. That is what they owe you for dinner. Also, if you are single order a take out.

If you picked Q: You do not get anything. Bye.

If you picked A: Your significant other owes you 50$. So what that they did no consent to this game. It is what is is!

THAT. If you won't complete your pet will die. YES I DID game. shot of hot sauce. Do not cheat. You chose to play this *If you picked J:* Sorry, unfortunately you have to chug a

If you picked 10: You must take 2 whole shots of your favorite liquor.

Pg.159

ALCOHOL DRINKS 4 U

SEX ON YOUR MOTHERS DRIVEWAY

WHAT TO GET
1 ounce peach schnapps
1 ounce blue curaçao
2 ounces vodka (or white rum)
Sprite

HOW TO MAKE IT
Put crushed ice in a highball glass. Pour in the ingredients, in order, ending by topping it off with Sprite. Stir and serve with a straw. Garnish with a lemon wheel.

THE INSANE UNICORN

WHAT TO GET
6 ounces Coconut Water
2 ounces Captain Morgan LocoNut
1/4 ounce grenadine
1/4 ounce Blue Curacao Liqueur
Edible purple glitter

HOW TO MAKE IT
Dip a 13 ounce highball glass in water and then edible glitter to form a rim. Fill the glass with ice. Add coconut water and Captain Morgan LocoNut. Stir until blended. Drizzle the Grenadine in slowly so it falls to the bottom and sits. Now slowly drizzle the Curacao in, so it sits on the top.

DAMN ITS A HURRICANE

WHAT TO GET
One part dark rum (2oz)
One part light rum (2oz)
Passion Fruit Syrup (1oz)
Juice of 1/2 lime
MIX IT ! DONE

Cocktail 6 oz. | Old-Fashioned 6½ oz. | White Wine 7¾ oz. | Highball 8 oz.

Blooming Onion

Serving: 4 Onions. **Prep Time:** 15 minutes. **Cook Time:** 15 minutes.

Get This:

- **3 eggs** - #DadJokeOfTheDay - *Why did the new egg feel so good? Because he just got laid!*
- **1 ½ cup milk** – I always wonder, if *SOY MILK* is just milk introducing itself in Spanish?
- **2 ½ cup flour** — My friends son told me this: I said to my teacher, *"I don't think I deserved zero for this exam."* She said, *"I agree, but I couldn't give you any less."* I did not know what to say!
- **2 teaspoon thyme** — How come *"you're a peach"* is a complement but *"you're bananas"* is an insult? Why are we allowing fruit discrimination to tear society apart?
- **2 teaspoon salt** — Kind of like your soul. Salty as heck. Do not deny it.
- **2 teaspoon ground cayenne pepper** - I got hit in the head with a can of Dr. Pepper today Luckily, I'm not hurt, it was a soft drink.
- **1 teaspoon ground black pepper** — Mmmm… nothing like a spicy sensation.
- **2 tablespoons paprika** — My grandpa got upset at my neighbor and said: *If I wanted to hear from an asshole, I'd fart.*
- **2 tablespoon cumin** — My neighbor goes: *David you cook so good. My girlfriend for example shes such a bad cook, she uses the smoke alarm as a timer.*
- **2 teaspoon dried oregano** — Dried, like my Italian friend's grandpa Giuseppe.
- **2 teaspoons garlic powder** —Your gene pool could use a little chlorine.
- **4 medium sweet onions** — My friend's kid goes: *My sister thought she was so smart; she said the only vegetable/fruit that can make her cry is a onion.* - So, I threw a coconut at her.

For the sauce:

- **1/2 teaspoon paprika** - #AnotherDadJokeOfTheDay - Two guys stole a calendar. They got six months each.
- **1/2 teaspoon garlic powder** – I may love to shop but I'm not buying your bullsh*t.
- **1/4 teaspoon ground cayenne pepper** – Also, If bullsh*t could float...you'd be the Admiral of the fleet!
- **1/4 cup mayonnaise** – Friend to her husband: *You're proof that god has a sense of humor.*
- **1/4 cup sour cream** – Take a shot!
- **1 1/2 tablespoons creamy horseradish** – When I was young this kid pi*sed me off. I made a poem for him: *Roses are red, Violets are blue. I've got five fingers, The middle one is for you.*
- **1 1/2 tablespoons ketchup** – You can't ketchup, can you?

Do This:

Combine: mayonnaise, horseradish, sour cream, ketchup, paprika, cayenne pepper and garlic powder in a bowl.

NOW, whisk eggs and milk in a separate bowl wide and deep enough to dunk the onion.

Mix: flour, cumin, paprika, dried oregano, salt, thyme, cayenne pepper, black pepper and garlic powder in another bowl wide enough to fit the onion.

CUT a small flat spot on the none root end of our onion. Remove any dried or damaged peels. Place our onion flat side down on a cutting board (root side up). Using a sharp knife starting about 1/2 inch from the root make a clean slice downward. Turn the onion one quarter turn and make another clean slice downward. Then, follow that with two more quarter turns and two more clean slices downward. Cut three to four equal spaced cuts downward in each of those four sections. Then turn the onion root side down and gently fan out the sections. TO SIMPLIFY LIKE THIS:

NOW dunk the onion in the bowl with the flour mixture. Coat the onion with the flour mixture spreading and separating the onion to make sure that it all gets breaded. Now dunk the onion into the egg mixture. Then back into the flour mixture.

HEAT oil in a deeper pot to 380 degrees. You will need just enough oil to cover the onion. Fry the onions root side up for 5-7 minutes. Drain on paper towels. Serve with the dipping sauce.

Disclaimer: You might get addicted to this. *

Take a shot you deserve it!

Unless you are under 21. Juice box for you honey!

Pg. 163

Avocadonator Devilled Eggsies

Serving: 12 devilled eggs.

Prep Time: 5 minutes.

Cook Time: I mean mixing time 2 min.

Get This:

- **6 hardboiled eggs cut in half** – #DadJokeOfTheDay *What is the difference between you - my dear and an egg?* Eggs get laid you do not.
- **2 large avocados** - #AnotherDadJokeOfTheDay - *What's an avocado's favorite music?* Guac N' Roll!
- **4 tsp lime juice** – My friend goes to her husband: *Everyone brings happiness to a room. I do when I enter, you do when you leave.* He didn't wait long to reply and said: *I'm visualizing duct tape over your mouth. I would smack you, but that would be animal abuse.* They had been married for quite some time. How? IDK!
- **2 tsp cilantro** – Once, my teacher pointed his ruler at me when I was talking in class and told me there was an idiot at the end of it. I asked which end. *Yours?* We all knew it Sherlock…. I got detention! Haha.
- **4 Slices of fried crushed bacon** – My grandpa goes: *How do you get to the top of a weather beacon?* Me: *How?* Him: *Climate...* Now I know why grandpa never became a comedian.
- **½ cup of chopped fresh parsley** - *What is green, and sings???* Elvis Parsley OF COURSE!
- **Pinch of garlic powder salt and pepper, Sprinkle with paprika.**

Do This:

BOIL the eggs until they are done. Around 8-15 mins. Remove the shells from the hard-boiled eggs. Slice the peeled eggs lengthwise and carefully remove the cooked yolks, placing the yolks in a mixing bowl. Cut avocado in half, take the insides out.

ADD avocado to the bowl and mash with a fork until it is a smooth consistency. Then add the remaining ingredients and mash stir together until blended. Spoon the mixture into the egg halves. Then sprinkle with paprika, fresh parsley and becon.

JALAPENO CHEESE BALLZ
NO BAKING NEEDED

Serving: 15 – 20 BALLZ.

Prep Time: 15 minutes.

Cook Time: Mixing time 5-10 mins.

 Did someone ask for tequila?

Get This.

- *2 tablespoons minced fresh chives* – DadJokeOfTheDay: crush: *how much do you love me??* me: *well look at the stars outside.* crush: *but its morning.* me: *exactly.*

- *¼ cup minced jalapeño, seeded* – My friend goes to her husband: *You are like a cloud. When you go away, it's a beautiful day.* His response to her was: *Light travels faster than sound. Therefore, some people appear bright until you hear them speak like you.*

- *1 cup sharp white cheddar, shredded* – My friend's kid goes: *My older teacher asked me today "If I say, 'I am beautiful', which tense is that?"* I then replied: *"It's obviously past."* She did not seem happy.

- *2 small shallots minced* - R.I.P Shallots – you will be minced. Get it?

- *1-pound bacon* - #AnotherDadJokeOfTheDay: *What is the name of the movie about Bacon?* - Hamlet

- *12-ounces plain cream cheese softened* - Plain, just like your love life. Ouch.

- *1 ½ tablespoon sour cream* - Next door neighbor goes: *All of my relationships experiences are inside out Sour Patch Kids - Sweet, sour, gone.* Poor guy!

- *¼ teaspoon coarse salt* - What did pepper get arrested for? Well, an A-SALT!

- *¼ teaspoon garlic powder* - My friend asked her husband: *"What do you like the most in me: my pretty face or my sexy body?"* He looked at her from head to toe and replied: *"I like your sense of humor."* I never laughed so much.

- *¼ teaspoon onion powder* - You know, a parent's job is basically a daily struggle to help a crazy person stay alive.

FLIP THE BOOK UPSIDE_DOWN

¡ןnɟıʇnɐǝq ǝɹɐ no⅄

Do This:

GET a large skillet out and set it over medium-low heat, cook the bacon until crispy, about 9-12 minutes, and then set aside on a paper towel-lined plate to soak up any excess oil. You don't want cholesterol. Once cooled, crush the bacon and place it in a wide shallow bowl.

GET a large bowl, mix: cream cheese, sour cream, chives, jalapenos, cheddar, shallots, salt, garlic powder, and onion powder until thoroughly combined. Season to taste with salt and then refrigerate for at least 25 minutes.

USING a tablespoon or small cookie scoop as your guide, portion out a small amount of the filling and form it into a ball. Roll the cheese ball through the bacon and repeat until all the mixture is gone. Refrigerate until you're ready to serve. VOILA!

*_Disclaimer:_ If this was complicated for you. Please reach out for help. *

Are you happy with the result?

👍 YES ☐

👎 NO ☐

Do not worry I have one for you too!
If you are under 21 - drink glass of water child.

The Chipster Dip

Serving: It is a dip. IDK however many chips until you run out.

Prep Time: 10 mins

Cook Time: About 5 min.

Get This:

1 Cream cheese – #DadJokeOfTheDay: *What is cream cheese's favorite part of a wedding?* Well, The Toast.

1 Can of refried beans – *You are about to fart your life away. Beans do that....*

1 ½ cup of salsa – *I usually use medium but you do what you want. Salsa in that isle!*

1 cup of Shredded Cheddar & Mozzarella – My friend's kid got suspended today. Apparently, this is what happened:

Teacher: *"Kids, what does the chicken give you?"*
Kid: *"Meat!"*
Teacher: *"Very good! Now what does the pig give you?"*
Kid: *"Bacon!"*
Teacher: *"Great! And what does the fat cow give you?"*
Kid: *"Homework!"*
I mean kid got jokes!

Favorite tortilla chips.

Do not forget the chips!

Do This:

GET a baking pan out. The smaller kind. Add refried beans as a first bottom layer. Melt cream cheese in a microwave for about 1 minute then spread it on top of the refried beans.

NEXT layer is salsa. You can use 1 ½ or more depends on your taste.

FINALLY top it with shredded cheese. Bake for 6 minutes on 350F.

*__Disclaimer:__ This is easy but damn good. *

Pg.167

Them Chick'n Sliders

Serving: 12 chicken sliders.

Prep Time: 1 hour *(marinading)*.

Cook Time: 12 minutes.

Get This:

- **3 tablespoons of salt, sugar, unsalted butter** – Each separate!
- **2 tablespoons black pepper** - #DadJokeOfTheDay: *Why did the teacher marry the janitor?* He swept her off her feet.
- **1/4 teaspoon cayenne pepper** - When I was a toddler, my parents would always say, *"Excuse my French"* just after a swear word. I will never forget the first day at school when my teacher asked if any of us knew any French. Man was she surprised.
- **1/2 teaspoon garlic powder** - Your breath about to smell!
- **3 large boneless skinless chicken breasts, cut crosswise into 4 pieces each** - 0 Jokes!
- **1 tablespoon paprika** - My married single friend said this: *At my age I am no longer a snack; I'm a Happy Meal. I come with toys and kids.*
- **1 cup milk** - My neighbor to his kid: *You're the reason god created the middle finger.*
- **2 large eggs** - This lady to her husband: *You're so sad that even Bob the Builder can't fix your life.*
- **1 1/2 cups all purpose flour** - All-purpose like you neighbor Linda.
- **4 tablespoons powdered non-fat milk** - If I could meet my brain the first thing I would probably say is: "It was truly and sincerely horrible working with you."
- **1 1/2 teaspoons baking powder & teaspoons baking soda** – Each separate!
- **2 quarts peanut or vegetable oil** - Either one will do!
- **12 dill pickle chips & 12 mini burger buns** - My teacher once told me I failed my exam. I told her she failed to educate me.

Sandwich Sauce:

- **1 cup of mayo** – #AnotherDadJokeOfTheDay - *What do you call a laughing jar of mayonnaise?* LMAYO
- **1 cup of BBQ sauce of choice** - Any would do. I usually choose the average basic BBQ sauce.
- **½ cup of mustard of choice** – Any mustard. I used spicy one. It was bomb.
- **½ cup of pickle juice** – This is important. This is what makes this sauce… The banger!
- **2 TBS of garlic powder** – Once my mom told me garlic makes everything better… So, I sprinkled it at my parents' marriage certificate…. You have guessed it did not work instead – they divorced.

Do This:

For the Chickn':

COMBINE salt and sugar with 1 quart room temperature water, whisk until dissolved. Add chicken and refrigerate for as little as 1 ½ hour and up to 2.

NOW: combine paprika, cayenne pepper, black pepper and garlic powder in a small bowl. Set aside. Whisk together milk and eggs in a medium bowl. Set aside.

COMBINE flour, non-fat milk powder, baking powder, 1 tablespoon kosher salt and 1 tablespoon of spice mixture in a large bowl and whisk to combine.

ADD 4 tablespoons milk/egg mixture into flour mixture and rub with fingertips until the flour mixture is coarse like wet sand. Feels nasty I know. In a large pot heat oil on high.

NOW, remove chicken breasts from brine and pat dry with paper towels. Season on both sides with spice mixture. Dip in milk mixture, then transfer to flour mixture. Turn to coat, pressing on the chicken to get as much of the flour mixture as you can on the cutlet. Shake off excess flour, then place onto a rack set over a sheet pan. Repeat with remaining chicken until it is all coated.

COOK turning breasts occasionally until golden brown and crisp on all sides, and chicken is cooked through, about 3-4 minutes total. Transfer to a paper plate. Melt 1 tablespoon of butter in a large skillet and toast split buns until golden brown, working in batches and adding more butter as needed. Plate a pickle on the bottom bun, cover with a piece of chicken top with the sauce you had made!

*_Disclaimer:_ This will rock your party! You are welcome! *

Instructions:

Find 3 words. They will describe your future. If you are not satisfied - take a shot. If you are satisfied also take a shot. Win-Win.

LETS PLAY A GAME

E	X	I	V	A	M	A	Z	I	N	G	R	M	E
S	D	V	O	E	E	I	L	I	I	S	C	E	E
A	D	A	T	P	O	A	I	R	L	N	P	O	X
E	N	C	R	O	I	U	D	O	S	R	A	E	L
H	E	A	A	O	Z	C	V	E	U	D	D	S	D
T	S	T	G	R	O	E	N	R	C	E	V	N	A
R	R	I	I	Y	D	C	O	I	C	P	E	M	L
S	N	O	C	C	X	R	R	A	E	R	N	E	T
S	R	N	A	Z	G	S	L	N	S	E	T	I	A
C	R	I	I	N	S	T	U	O	S	S	U	R	E
S	E	T	C	N	S	A	D	I	F	S	R	A	S
E	E	O	E	H	C	C	D	L	U	E	E	V	T
X	A	H	T	A	Z	R	C	I	L	D	I	H	T
Y	M	C	R	E	L	A	X	M	I	A	S	S	G

The Avocado Emperor Toast

Serving: 4 Toasts. **Prep Time:** 10 minutes. **Cook Time:** 10 minutes

Get This:

4 slices of your favorite bread – #DadJokeOfTheDay - *Why did the loaf of bread break up with his girlfriend? The relationship was crumbling.*

½ cup of freshly chopped parsley - #AnotherDadJokeOfTheDay - *If parsley were a singer what would be his name? Elvis Parsley of course!*

4 large eggs – My friend's kid is a jokester! Kid has some jokes. The other day he got mad at his older brother and said: *You are so dumb that when you were driving to Disneyland you saw a sign that said "Disneyland Left" so you turned around and went home.*

8 slices of fried and crunched bacon – I was once at the store and this lady got upset at a cashier, he didn't take her crap and said: *You must have been born on a highway because that's where most accidents happen.* I clapped!

2 Large avocados – Oh my gosh. Going back to my friend's kid. Once he asked his grandma how old grandpa is. His grandma said: *He is so old that he owes Moses a dollar. Also, so old that his tax file number is 1.*

Salt/pepper to taste.

Do This:

IN a bowl mash all avocados with salt and pepper. Take out a pan, add some oil and fry all 4 eggs. Set aside.

NOW take your bread and toast it so its crispy. Then spread your avocado on all pieces. Add egg on each one. Top with fresh parsley and crunched bacon. Pair with a mimosa.

*__Disclaimer:__ This is a quick delicious recipe! You can also try without the egg *

Quick Mimosa:
½ cup of orange juice, ½ cup of cranberry juice, 1 cup of champagne. Mix, Chug!

K. Bye

The End

Thai: ปลาย
Turkish: son
Uzbek: oxiri
Vietnamese: kết thúc

Welsh: diwedd
Xhosa: isiphelo
Ukrainian: кінець
Yiddish: סוף *Tamil:* இறுதியில்
Yoruba: opin
Zulu: ukuphela

Afrikaans: einde
Albanian: fund
Amharic: ማብቂያ
Arabic: النهاية *Urdu:* اختتام
Armenian: պէտք
Azerbaijani: son
Basque: end
Belarusian: канец
Bengali: শেষ
Bosnian: kraj   *Greek:* τέλος
Bulgarian: край
Catalan: final
Cebuano: katapusan
Chichewa: TSIRIZA
Chinese (Simplified): 结束
Chinese (Traditional): 結束
Corsican: fine
Croatian: kraj
Czech: konec
Danish: ende
Dutch: einde
English: end
Esperanto: fino
Estonian: lõpp
Filipino: wakas
Finnish: pää
French: fin
Frisian: ein
Galician: final
Georgian: დასასრული
German: Ende

Gujarati: અંત
Haitian Creole: fen
Hausa: karshen
Hawaiian: hopena
Hebrew: ח
Hindi: समाप्त
Hmong: kawg
Hungarian: vég
Icelandic: enda
Igbo: njedebe
Indonesian: akhir
Irish: deireadh
Italian: fine
Japanese: 終わり
Javanese: pungkasan
Kannada: ಅಂತ್ಯ
Kazakh: Соңы
Khmer: បញ្ចប់
Korean: 종료
Kurdish (Kurmanji): dawî
Kyrgyz: Бир мезгилдин акырына карата
Lao: ສົ້ນສຸດ
Latin: finis
Latvian: beigas
Lithuanian: pabaiga
Luxembourgish: Enn
Macedonian: крајот
Malagasy: tapitra
Malay: akhir
Malayalam: അവസാനി ക്കുന്നു

Maltese: tmiem
Maori: mutunga
Marathi: शेवट
Mongolian: Төгсгөл
Myanmar (Burmese): အဆုံး
Nepali: अन्त
Norwegian: SLUTT - my fav!
Pashto: پای
Persian: پایان
Polish: koniec
Portuguese: fim
Punjabi: ਅੰਤ
Romanian: Sfârșit
Russian: конец
Samoan: iuga
Scots Gaelic: deireadh
Serbian: крај
Sesotho: qeta
Shona: kuguma
Sindhi: آخر
Sinhala: අවසානය
Slovak: koniec
Slovenian: koncu
Somali: dhammaad
Spanish: fin
Sundanese: tungtung
Swahili: mwisho
Swedish: SLUT -it's real.
Tajik: Поён
Telugu: ముగింపు

It is sadly the END
It was nice cooking with you.

FUN TIP:
If you want to have a cute date. Tell your partner/friend to open the book and go page by page while you have your eyes closed. When you say stop while they flip pages – whatever page you stop on – that is your dinner date.

From me:

Hello, thank you for buying this book – if you did not buy it – *GOODBYE!* Of course, I am joking. You maybe received it as a gift or stole it from someone. *Who knows?* Either or, if this book is in your possession, you are one lucky person, or hunted by me. I wrote this book, did photos, and designed it page by page by myself. It took loads of effort, lots of hours and lots of time! At the end, this was worth it as I can now share this with you. You can laugh a little loosen that BOTOX of yours or get fu*ked up while cooking. Unless you are under 21 then only water for you. Or you can suck on an ICE CUBE. Do not hate me kids under 21. I had been in your shoes. I mention alcohol a lot in this book – which is ironic as I myself do not drink that much. I know *BOO DAVID GET OFF THE STAGE!* … I get it… If you know my friends, they will assure you that 2 drinks and David is drunk! I want to thank everyone who supported this journey *(you know who you are)*. I wish you all the best! Once you are done with this book! PASS IT ALONG to someone. Create a chain! Why not. Last stupid joke: *How did the MP3 file say goodbye to the other music files..?* Audios. On that note! Goodbye, it was fun cooking with you. I'm sure few of you used this book inappropriately… For those who used it for cooking I am sure you smacked my face at least once… Or draw a mustache… I would not be surprised. Last one goodbye! Now let us take a farewell shot of goodbye... *NO NOT YOU KIDS under 21. Get a juice-box.*
Oh before I forget! If there are any mistakes.. I am sorry I am a human and we could of made an error. If you wish to complain about it you have 170 pages with my face on it. Give *me a facepalm..Or slap me I whatever.*

Made in the USA
Middletown, DE
18 December 2022